What's so great about the Eiffel Tower?

LAURENCE KING

Published in 2017 by Laurence King Publishing Ltd
361–373 City Road
London EC1V 1LR
Tel +44 20 7841 6900
Fax +44 20 7841 6910
E enquiries@laurenceking.com
www.laurenceking.com

A catalogue record for this book is available from the British Library

ISBN 978 178067 919 8

Designed by The Urban Ant
Cover design by Charlie Bolton
Project editor: Gaynor Sermon
Commissioning editor: Liz Faber
Picture researcher: Peter Kent
Printed in China

What's so great about the Eiffel Tower?

70 questions that will change the way you think about architecture

Jonathan Glancey

LAURENCE KING PUBLISHING

Contents

Introduction

'The days of our years', say the Psalms, 'are threescore years and ten'. The sky-piercing spire of Salisbury Cathedral is 700 years old, the Great Pyramid of Giza is almost seven times as old, while the temple at the heart of Eridu – possibly the world's first city – rose in tiers of baked mud bricks from the long-silted gulf shores of what is today southern Iraq some 7,000 years ago.

If human life can seem all too short, that of architecture can be very long indeed. And because buildings endure, the ways they are looked at, thought about and discussed by succeeding generations tends to change over time. In early eighteenth-century England, for example, clean-cut young Palladian architects and polemicists, led by Lord Burlington, spurned what they saw as the vulgarity of the masterly Baroque designs of Christopher Wren, John Vanbrugh and Nicholas Hawksmoor.

Nineteenth-century neo-Goths, in hock to a make-believe view of life in medieval Europe, considered all classically inspired design, Wren or Burlington, untruthful, unpatriotic and pagan. Spires good: domes and regimented facades bad. In their turn, Gothic Revivalists were demonized by rational young functionalists after World War I when clinical, white Modern architecture disinfected and purified age-old city streets.

By the 1970s, Modernism was on the ropes, as conservationists and Post-Moderns took to the ring. And so it has gone on, with historians continually updating and revising architectural history and critics turning on proverbial sixpences to justify now one style of design, now another, with equal zeal.

Today, it seems hard to believe that, just half a century ago, architects, planners and governments were hell bent on what they called 'comprehensive redevelopment', or what many of us think of as the wholesale destruction of old town and city centres and their historic buildings, and their replacement with millions of cubic feet of mostly low-grade concrete design.

I have just used the term 'hell bent' to evoke an era when a spirit of largely unmitigated modernization breathed heavily on cities worldwide. My choice of words is loaded. In the 1960s, modernizers felt they were making exactly the *right* choices. They thought of themselves as leading us all to the New Jerusalem – heaven, not hell. Today, in the second decade of the twenty-first century, my 'hell bent' might be questionable to those nostalgic for the world of 1960s concrete, flyovers, heavy-handed state intervention and Brutalist architecture that defied conventional notions of good taste.

So, where I see the recent renovation of the interior of Chartres Cathedral as anathema, stripping away irreplaceable layers of history, others will see it as a loving recreation of how Chartres looked in its medieval heyday. History itself, of course, is a construct, patched up, renovated and rewritten to suit the prevailing tastes, ideas and conceits of different generations.

The judgements we make at any one time in history deserve to be questioned. It was not long ago, for example, that we were told – as if this was gospel truth – that the Egyptian pyramids were built by slaves rather than free men. Now, we are not even sure if the Great Pyramid of Giza ever housed the mummified corpse of the pharaoh who is said to have commissioned it.

So, here are 70 questions – one for each year of our biblically allotted lifespan – to ask of architecture through history and around the world. Great buildings and engineering structures that, like the Eiffel Tower, have influenced the art and science of architecture are mostly here to stay, yet how we see them will continue to change with winds, tides and passing fashions and philosophies.

Jonathan Glancey

Parthenon
Cold formalism or classical exuberance?

In 1832, Otto, a Bavarian prince, became the first king of a newly independent Greece and declared Athens its capital when the city was little more than a ramshackle huddle of a few hundred Ottoman houses clustered around the ruins of the Acropolis. Otto commissioned a new city plan, and within a decade grand new Greek Revival buildings commanded handsome streets and squares. The style of architecture was rational, severe, even militaristic. Here was ancient Athens revived through a distinctly Germanic lens.

Otto's father, Ludwig I of Bavaria, was an ardent Hellenophile who believed in the essential purity and chasteness of Greek art and architecture. He imagined the temples and public buildings of fifth-century Athens to have been as white as the snow that fell on the Bavarian Alps and, as the influential eighteenth-century German art historian Johann Joachim Winckelmann had put it, 'the whiter the building is, the more beautiful it is as well'. In Bavaria, Ludwig had commissioned his court architect, Leo von Klenze, to build a replica of the Parthenon. Overlooking the Danube beyond Regensburg, this nineteenth-century national Valhalla, devoted to the eternal memory of great Germans, appeared as chaste and as monochromatic as any contemporary military fortification.

This particular interpretation of Greek architecture as heroic and in the service of a clean-cut and highly ordered society was conflated with the belief that the great buildings of ancient Athens were made of pure, unadorned marble. And this is why the monumental architecture of the Greek Revival that flourished from the late eighteenth century across Europe, its empires and the Americas, was as severe and, yes, as Germanic as its appears.

And yet, in actual fact, ancient Athens and the Parthenon were cinematically colourful. Designed by the architects Ictinus and Callicrates, with the sculptor and painter Phidias, the city's greatest building – the Parthenon – was built and decorated between 447 and 431 BCE at the height of Athenian power.

Coloured detail by Gottfried Semper, 1836

Ο ΔΗΜΟΣ   ΣΕ ΕΝ ΤΟΓ   ΩΝ
ΑΘΗΝΑΙΟΣ   ΛΙΤΟΥΓΑΙ   ΡΕ
ΚΑΤΕΣΚΕΥΛ   ΛΙΟΥ ΓΑΡΘΕΝ   ΤΟ

Its architecture was perfectly proportioned, and adorned with a restless frieze of relief sculpture of the very highest order. These depicted mythical battles between the Greeks and their ancient enemies, gods and giants, centaurs, Trojans and Amazons and, like the pediments and interior of this sublime temple, were brightly coloured.

To add to the richness of its symbolism, the Parthenon was aligned with the constellation Hyades (in mythology, the daughters of Atlas, the titan who held up the celestial spheres and was associated with the stars and navigation). Its subtly curved fluted columns gave the building something of the look of a great warship, its sails billowing with favourable winds, while if they could be projected into the heavens, the temple's 46 outer columns would meet at a point a mile into the Aegean sky, pointing towards the heavenly sisters. Here, myth, meaning, art and architecture were intertwined and decidedly colourful.

Dedicated to the Virgin goddess Athena, the Parthenon's future would be equally colourful. In 435 CE, Theodosius II, emperor of the Eastern Roman Empire, closed and looted the Greek temples and, some decades later, the Parthenon was rededicated as an Orthodox church, the Parthenon Maria, in honour of the Virgin Mary. In later centuries, with Athens under the control of Latin kingdoms, the Doric temple became a Roman Catholic Church, with a bell tower added to its southwest corner.

Contemporary ruins of the Parthenon

Some while after Athens was swallowed by the Ottoman Empire in 1458, the bell tower was transformed into a minaret as the Parthenon became a mosque. When the Venetians launched an attack on Ottoman Athens in 1687, the Turks used the temple-mosque as an ammunition store. It received a direct hit from Venetian guns. The roof was blown off along with most of the frieze. Six columns were demolished along with the cella, or interior of the temple. The Parthenon was now, more or less, the ruin we know today. More or less because, when the Venetians turned for home, the Ottomans built a small, provincial-style mosque within the ruins. And this is how matters rested until Greek independence, the clearing of Ottoman buildings from the Acropolis, and the sanitizing of architecture and history to fit an essentially German Neoclassical ideal.

As late as 1877, when the painter Lawrence Alma-Tadema first exhibited his colourful *Phidias Showing the Frieze of the Parthenon to his Friends*, there was no consensus on the issue of Greek architecture and colour. Dedicated Neoclassicists were certain that the Greeks had more noble and Germanic tastes, while Romantics like Alma-Tadema knew differently – and were proved right.

Even then, when in 1911 the young Charles-Édouard Jeanneret first set eyes on the Parthenon, he was struck by the way the Mediterranean sunlight played on the 'harsh poetry' of the ruins. 'Never in my life', wrote the future Le Corbusier, 'have I experienced the subtleties of such monochromy.' There it was again: the Parthenon as a stark monument that, fascinatingly, would resonate in the future architect's radical twentieth-century architecture. I wonder what Le Corbusier would have made of the full-scale replica of the Parthenon built in Nashville for the Tennessee Centennial Exposition of 1897? The original temporary structure was realized in plaster, brick and wood, and later reconstructed in concrete (the Swiss-French architect's favourite material) rather than marble.

The history of the Parthenon shows how a specific building has different meanings and values for different cultures and generations. And yet, whether a feast of colour and life, or an exquisite monochrome art-historical monument, it can never be ignored.

Venice

Architectural museum or living city?

'We repudiate the old Venice', declared Filippo Tommaso Marinetti, the Italian poet, editor and founder of the Futurist movement, in 1910. A year earlier, his *Futurist Manifesto* had been dedicated to speed, war, industry and the subjugation of women. His latest work was now being strewn, in thousands of handbills, from the top of the Renaissance clock tower in St Mark's Square.

'We want to cure and heal this putrefying city, this magnificent sore from the past … let us hasten to fill in its little reeking canals with the ruins from its leprous and crumbling palaces. Let us burn the gondolas – rocking chairs for cretins – and raise to the heavens the imposing geometry of metal bridges and factories plumed with smoke, to abolish the cascading curves of the old architecture.'

In 1910, Venice remained deaf to such iconoclastic pleas. Although new bridges and factories were built – mostly in Mestre on the far side of the railway bridge linking 'La Serenissima' to the mainland – strident Futurism and nascent Modernism were to make little headway in this great dowager duchess of a city.

Grand Canal, Venice, looking towards Salute and Punta della Dogana

Marinetti, however, did have some impact. After World War I, the poet fell in with Benito Mussolini and wrote the *Fascist Manifesto* of 1919. And, although Mussolini was no dogmatist when it came to architecture, he did endow Venice with the impressive Ponte Littorio, the dual-carriageway road bridge linking the city to the mainland, along with a cinema, casino, new housing and an airport on the Lido.

Preservation, though, has been the driving force of most architectural endeavour in Venice since John Ruskin drew and measured buildings here and railed against the arrival of steam trains in 1846. Although no fan of Palladianism, Ruskin was shocked by the demolition of the church of Santa Lucia – Andrea Palladio had made sketches for this before his death in 1580 – demanded by the construction of a railway terminus facing the Grand Canal.

Ever since, conservationists have battled the forces of Modernism. There have been those who have wanted to pickle the city in Ruskinian aspic, as if it was nothing more – or less – than one enormous antique artwork, and those who have agreed to change, as long as this is hidden away. As a result, many of the best Modern interventions in the city are interiors, and notably those of the inventive Venetian architect Carlo Scarpa. Among these are the exquisitely restored Olivetti showroom in St Mark's Square (1958),

Venice as global attraction: The Venetian Resort Hotel, Las Vegas

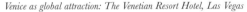

his work at the Fondazione Querini Stampalia (1959) – a beautiful house-museum with a magnificent historic art collection – and the Palazzo Fondazione Masieri, a research institute on the Grand Canal, completed after Scarpa's death in 1979.

The story of the Palazzo Fondazione Masieri takes us to the heart of the debate over Modernism in Venice. In 1952, Angelo Masieri, a 30-year-old architect, and his wife Savina went to Arizona to see Frank Lloyd Wright. They commissioned the legendary American architect to design a replacement for the family's palazzo on the corner of Rio Nuovo and the Grand Canal. Wright's design was modest and even respectful of Venetian tradition. Nevertheless, it unleashed a storm of protest. If it was built, roared Ernest Hemingway, Venice deserved to burn. Other influential voices agreed: the Wright palazzo was wrong for Venice. It was refused planning permission. The project was dead in the water. Angelo Masieri, too, was dead, killed in a road accident on his way to see Wright in the States.

As if to reinforce the conservationists' victory, two other distinguished Modern architects came to grief in Venice in the 1960s – Le Corbusier, with a design for a hospital in Cannaregio, and Louis Kahn, with a conference centre in the Arsenale, the city's medieval shipyard. Both projects died here.

Ever since, Venice has embraced Modern architecture as long as venerable walls have veiled it. Tadao Ando's interior remodelling of the Punta della Dogana for the François Pinault collection of contemporary art (2009) is exemplary. Rem Koolhaas, meanwhile, has been working on and off for years on a controversial scheme to convert the imposing Fondaco dei Tedeschi by the Rialto Bridge into a shopping mall and cultural theme park for Benetton.

On the fringes of the old city there is new housing that is modern yet in keeping with the scale and grain of its surroundings, and yet wholly new buildings here are as rare as cars (much as Marinetti would have liked them roaring along a cemented-over Grand Canal), and when they do emerge – like Stirling and Wilford's Biennale bookshop pavilion (1991) in the Giardini – they are modest events.

Venice does not respond to loud futuristic or intense modern gestures, but to subtlety, secrecy and Scarpa. Although not quite a museum, it moves forwards and sideways with the caution and gait of the hermit crabs found along its shores.

Mies van der Rohe
Less is more or less is a bore?

Ludwig Mies van der Rohe (1886–1969) was one of the great architects of the twentieth century. His mature buildings achieved a level of cool, detached abstraction and near minimalism. And, yet, from the Barcelona Pavilion of 1929 to the Seagram Building, New York (1958), his work was also characterized by the use of rich materials and a high level of craftsmanship.

The son of an Aachen stonemason, Mies would declare, 'God is in the details' and 'Less is more'. By this, however, he did not mean soulless, clinical rectilinear buildings, but architecture refined to its well-detailed essence. His designs for the Friedrichstrasse skyscraper

The Barcelona Pavilion as recreated in 1986

competition of 1921–22, for example, showed him working towards a glass-and-steel architecture as natural and as beautiful as a crystal. Neither the technology nor the will existed to realize such designs at the time, yet worked up after the competition as display drawings using bold charcoal lines mixed with photomontage, Mies's schemes are anything but cold. They are full of contained energy from a tautly harnessed imagination.

And yet, drabness was the accusation levelled at Mies by his critics. In his provocative book, *Complexity and Contradiction in Architecture* (1966), the American Postmodern architect Robert Venturi declared 'Less is a bore', encouraging a cheap-shot reaction to the German-American architect's pared-down designs. It was no fault of Mies that so many clients, cities and lesser architects around the world chose to ape what they saw as an ahistorical style of architecture, ideally suited to the mass production of fast-buck office towers.

Mies's architecture had, in fact, drawn on history. His early projects were highly influenced by Neoclassicism, and in particular by the work of the Prussian architect Karl Friedrich Schinkel (1781–1841), while his sense of structure and feeling for materials reflected his close attachment to medieval architecture and masonry. As a child he would sit in awe, contemplating the vaults of Aachen Cathedral, and he revered Ewald, his elder brother, a highly skilled mason and stone carver.

Today, Mies has been rescued from infamy, and yet to understand the difference between the Seagram Building and a run-of-the-mill downtown office tower, or between the architect's 860–880 Lake Shore Drive apartment blocks and those rushed up in a superficially similar manner, requires an unprejudiced mind and wide-open eyes.

The Seagram Building, Manhattan, New York

St Paul's Cathedral

Baroque masterpiece or
Renaissance sham?

His hands were tied from the beginning, his fertile imagination reined in. When Christopher Wren was asked to design a replacement for St Paul's Cathedral – the original medieval building had been effectively destroyed by the Great Fire of London in 1666 – his clients, the Church Commissioners, were unsure how to move with the architectural times. When Wren proposed a magnificent domed cathedral based on a Greek-cross plan, they were aghast. What they really wanted was a medieval cathedral in fancy dress. In any case, Wren's ideal design could not have been built in affordable sections at a time: it was all of a very beautiful piece.

Wren went back to the drawing board and produced a hideous design for a cruciform cathedral with a tall and narrow dome and half-hearted Renaissance details that did a disservice to both his undoubted talent and to the Church of England itself. This, though, was the approved Warrant Design of 1675. If it had been built,

Wren's original cruciform design for St Paul's, as approved by his client

Wren's reputation would never have been what it deservedly has been. And yet, as the Wren family memoir, *Parentalia*, records, Wren was allowed 'the Liberty in the Prosecution of his Work' – granted by the King – 'to make some Variations, rather ornamental, than essential, as from Time to Time he should see proper; and to leave the Whole to his own Management.'

Ornamental indeed. Wren set about reworking the Warrant Design, so much so that when St Paul's was completed in 1710 it looked nothing like the approved design of 35 years earlier. It was a compromise, most certainly, but a magnificent and very English compromise. Renaissance walls raised high around a Gothic plan, concealed flying buttresses, and the most ingenious dome yet, devised using every trick known to late seventeenth-century structural engineering, worked together to shape a compelling Baroque cathedral.

And yet, accusations have echoed down the centuries, pointing a finger at St Paul's and saying its design is dishonest. How dare it hide its Gothic plan? Wren's genius, though – displayed during his long career – lay very often in his ability to adapt the noblest ideals to the reality of the laws of counting houses and views of clients quite unable (and to an extent, understandably so) to see how well their architect's work would endure in the very long term.

The serene dome of St Paul's, completed in 1710

Great Pyramid of Giza

*Overscaled royal tomb, or sublime
gateway to the cosmos?*

In essence, the Great Pyramid of Giza is simple enough: an
enormous man-made mountain built by a colossal workforce over
some 20 years as a tomb for the pharaoh Khufu (Cheops in Greek),
who died c. 2560 BCE. Hemiunu may have been the architect. At
146 metres (481 feet) high, the pyramid was the world's tallest
building until the completion, in 1311, of the spire (since lost) of
Lincoln Cathedral. And yet the only known image of Khufu is a 7.5-
cm- (3-inch-) high ivory figurine. A very much bigger statue of the
pharaoh's architect – more in keeping with the bulk of the pyramid
and its architectural ambition – can be seen in the Roemer-und-
Pelizaeus Museum, Hildesheim.

By any standards the Great Pyramid was a magnificent
achievement, and not least because the sheer scale and precision
of its construction have continued to baffle those who, even
today, cannot quite bring themselves to believe that ancient
civilizations, bereft of modern technology, could achieve so
much, so thoroughly well.

There is, though, much that continues to elude us. Was the
monument really for Khufu, a pharaoh of whom we know so little?
Why has no mummy ever been found in the pyramid? In 1983, Robert
Bauval, a structural engineer born and brought up in Alexandria,
put forward his Orion Correlation Theory: the Great Pyramid, and
indeed the entire complex at Giza, including the enigmatic Sphinx,
is a map of the constellations Orion and Leo and, by extension, of
the Milky Way. Light shafts spearing up from the 'King's Chamber'
at the heart of the Great Pyramid to the skies, point to stars in
Orion's Belt. The Egyptians associated Orion with Osiris, the god
of rebirth and the afterlife who, because of his own mythic death
and resurrection, was also associated with the annual flooding and
retreating of the Nile and, thus, the fertility of Egypt itself.

So, the Great Pyramid was always more important than the
life, death and increasingly dim memory of a single pharaoh who

may not even have been buried there. Bauval's theories have been dismissed by astronomers, geologists and historians, and yet it is very hard to look on this mighty structure – haunting at roseate dawn before armies of tourists arrive, and haunting again after dusk under an epiphany of stars – and believe that this was simply a tomb for a single and all but forgotten king.

Here, if anywhere, perhaps is an ancient star gate or, if not that, a highly accomplished, and once highly polished, monument that speaks loud, clear and poetically of the relative scales of human beings and eternity, of the immense yearnings of the human imagination, and of the collective will of an ancient civilization. Small wonder pyramids continue to haunt both the architectural and the popular imagination.

The Great Pyramid of Giza, with the Sphinx in the foreground

Stonehenge

International symbol or isolated monument?

This legendary circular monument on Salisbury Plain was rebuilt in stone at almost exactly the same time as the Egyptians raised the Great Pyramid of Giza. Both monuments appear to be linked to stars and solstices. Were they connected? Was an esoteric language passed along trade routes between the Nile Valley and Salisbury Plain?

While it is fascinating to think of both ancient Egyptians and Britons hauling huge stones weighing between 50 and 80 tonnes over long distances to build monuments that have survived the ages and that haunt us still, it is quite possible that these two cultures never met and that ideas for temples, tombs or places of gathering and possibly healing emerged in the guise of huge stone structures at much the same time in different parts of the world.

Current thinking suggests Stonehenge was created by a culture isolated from mainstream Europe, let alone North Africa, and that its alignment with the solstices was pre-ordained, given that the site on

Salisbury Plain does this naturally. Stonehenge owes far more to nature and sorcery than the Great Pyramid of Khufu. However, just as it is possible that the site of the temple and funerary complex at Giza dates back to as early as 10,000 BCE, so Stonehenge may well have existed in 8,000 BCE, although it would have been built in wood at the time.

In later years, Stonehenge would have been connected with Europe as travellers and traders made their way overland to what might have been a centre of healing or some common cultural bond. Close to the great upright stones, the bodies of people from as far as Germany have been identified. What seems certain is that, just as people come today in hope of some kind of spiritual happening or revelation on Salisbury Plain at solstice, so for very many generations people living during the Stone Age gathered here as part of a communion with sun, further stars and a sense of the infinite.

Significantly, perhaps, Stonehenge was least valued during the era of industrialization and scientific enquiry, when a price could be put on almost everything. In 1915, the site was auctioned at Salisbury's Palace Theatre by the estate agents Knight, Frank & Rutley. The hammer came down on 'Lot 15, Stonehenge, about 30 acres ...' at £6,600. Cecil Chubb, a Wiltshire businessman, bought it as a present for his wife. She was not amused. Chubb gave the site to the nation, receiving a knighthood in return.

Stonehenge, Salisbury Plain, Wiltshire

Chartres Cathedral

Labyrinth of sacred geometry,
or maze of ineffable kitsch?

On 16 August 1944, the US 7th Armored Division opened fire on the Cathedral of Notre Dame in Chartres. German snipers were said to be hiding in the western towers, with more troops inside. The order was given to destroy the medieval building. Just before this was carried out, Texan-born Colonel Welborn Barton Griffith Jr made a dash for the cathedral in company with a single enlisted soldier. Finding no enemy soldiers inside the cavernous building, Griffith rang the cathedral bells as a signal for his comrades to hold fire.

It had been a close-run thing. One of the greatest works of medieval architecture had been saved, although Griffith – awarded the US Distinguished Service Cross and several French honours – was killed the same day by German guns. The Germans, of course, might well have destroyed Chartres, too. At the time of the 1789 Revolution, even the French themselves had tried to destroy it.

After that, Chartres appeared to be in safe hands. And then, in 2009, the Monuments Historiques division of the French Ministry of Culture approved a monumentally expensive makeover of the cathedral that, in the eyes of many critics and visitors, has been sensationally destructive. Sensational is the *mot juste*: glorious, deep-grey walls aged over centuries have been painted and gilded in bright and garish colours, all creamy white, glossy yellow and *trompe l'oeil* marbling.

Where once the cathedral's peerless collection of medieval stained-glass windows punctuated the numinously sombre nave, chancel transepts and ambulatory with hallowed light, today they seem remarkably lacklustre in effect now that the walls are so luridly bright. For Adrien Goetz of *Le Figaro*, the new effect of stained glass in painted walls is like 'watching a film in a movie theatre where they haven't turned off the lights'.

Looking towards the chancel, Chartres Cathedral

Writing in the *New York Review of Books*, the American critic Martin Filler has likened the overarching new TV-makeover-show look for Chartres to 'some funeral parlour in Little Italy'. Frédéric Didier, the restoration architect, and his team talk of restoring the cathedral's original thirteenth-century decor – the project was due to be completed in 2017 – yet as Filler remarked, this is 'a pursuit as foolhardy as adding a head to the *Winged Victory of Samothrace* or arms to the *Venus de Milo*'.

It is impossible today to recreate the look and feel, or spirit, of the cathedral as it was in the thirteenth century. What was so special about Chartres is that it had remained all of a piece, despite the French revolutionaries and German and American soldiers in World War II. A sublime whole, it was built in a remarkably short time – for the most part between 1194 and 1230 – and, until 2009, had matured and aged more subtly than the finest French wines.

Garish modern makeover of the chancel

The combination of its sacred geometry, ancient stones pierced by haunting coloured light and sense of intense spirituality that made it so special has now been lost forever. It seems a wonder that the Ministry of Culture has, as yet, failed to send the cathedral's most famous relic – the cloak of the Virgin Mary – to a laundry for cleaning, or turned its compelling labyrinth, set into the floor, into a theme-park ride.

From the late twentieth century, shopping malls have been the cathedrals of the modern age, with theme parks, leisure centres and airport terminals as their attendant churches and chapels. Everything must be shiny, over-lit, antiseptic, supremely tacky and, above all, soulless. Chartres has been made to follow suit, to become a government-funded and approved religious playpen and tourist attraction, and in the process a credo to a lost cause: that of patina and a sense of history. It is an insult to the building, but also to the memory of Colonel Welborn Barton Griffith Jr, and the spirit of all those who have prayed or simply lost themselves in contemplation here over so many hundreds of years.

One of the great joys of old or ancient buildings is their very antiquity. Not just the age of their stones or timbers, that is, but their patina: the evidence of cathedral walls lit for centuries by tapers and candles, the sheen on stone from countless hands that have brushed along them, from the bodies that have passed along them. Worn steps and flagstones. Faded frescoes. Darkness visible. All of this is lost forever when restorationists who believe that they know better than history itself turn venerable places of worship into venal playpens for passing coach parties.

Manhattan Skyline
Ancient or modern?

Although other cities have grown bigger, higher and shinier than New York, the Manhattan skyline remains compelling. The cinematic sight of the Empire State Building soaring up from Midtown still stirs the imagination. The loss of the twin towers of the World Trade Center remains almost palpable 15 years on from the atrocity that brought them down, igniting wars, invasions and ever increasing terrorism that, loss of life aside, has seen historic monuments wilfully destroyed in God's name.

And yet, although terrorists destroyed the World Trade Center because, to them, it represented the modern Western world in Babel-like towers of concrete, steel and glass, Manhattan is a curiously old-fashioned place. Rising from a bed of solid granite, its many towers and spires are like man-made peaks, divided by gullies in the guise of a grid of streets and avenues, traffic flowing through them like torrents of water. Deep shadows cast along these artificial gullies, and fierce winds ripping along them in winter, add to a feeling that here is a geological formation as much as a modern city.

Even then Manhattan can appear as old as the hills. The island is linked to the mainland by hulking bridges, riveted and rusting, and lined not with skyscrapers alone but also with countless single-storey shacks, chiaroscuro depots and warehouses, serpentine fire hydrants, venerable water towers, antique emergency stairs and the kind of family shops, diners and delicatessens that have vanished from all too many modern cities.

These island avenues and streets resound with noises – the honking of fire tenders, the hiss of air brakes – reminiscent of those of ancient beasts. Le Corbusier found Manhattan somehow archaic, too, its buildings not big enough, by which he meant their scale or floor plan rather than their height. Despite the gridded, rational logic of its street plan, individual buildings shoot up from small plots like latter-day versions of the medieval tower houses of San Gimignano, or the church spires that once clustered around St Paul's Cathedral. The net effect is that of a medieval city reconsidered in the era of steel frames, elevators and electricity.

And yet, here lies a part of the allure of Manhattan. It might boast hundreds of tall buildings and yet these tend to meet streets in a notably humane way, with the frontages of even the tallest, including the Empire State Building, crowded with everyday shops and places to wolf down today's bargain-priced lunchtime special.

Mid-Manhattan skyline from the Hudson River

Sagrada Família

Genius or gimcrackery?

'My client is in no hurry.' Antoni Gaudí believed God had all the time in the world, so there was no need to rush the design and construction of the Sagrada Família. This is not Barcelona's cathedral, but the Basilica and Expiatory Temple of the Holy Family, an extraordinary and even bewildering building that has been under construction since 1882. When completed, probably some time this century, the highest of its 18 spires will soar 170 metres (560 feet) above the grid of nineteenth-century streets below. The Sagrada Família will be the world's tallest and most controversial church.

Paid for entirely by private donations and entrance fees from millions of visitors over three centuries, its unprecedented appearance has confused, disturbed, and divided the opinions of critics. For George Orwell it was 'one of the most hideous buildings in the world'; the English author prayed it would be destroyed during the Spanish Civil War. Louis Sullivan, the American 'father of skyscrapers', described it as 'spirit symbolized in stone', and Salvador Dalí said the building had a 'terrifying and edible beauty' and should be kept under a glass dome.

When the mind-numbingly complex stone vault over the 45.7-metre- (150-foot-) high nave was completed in 2010, the debate was reignited. According to Manuel Vicent, a columnist for the Madrid daily *El País*, 'The only saving grace of the Temple of the Sagrada Família was the fact that it was unfinished, the dream of a genius driven crazy by mystic reveries. Now it will be completed with the money of tourism, and when its walls are finally enclosed, there will be no one inside but Japanese tourists.'

Those who take against the Sagrada Família do so largely because they refuse to see beyond its richly decorated and apparently arbitrary forms. Scratch the surface, though, and this mind-bending building proves to be a tour de force of highly sophisticated mathematics and advanced structural engineering.

Vegetable-like stone towers of the Sagrada Família

Gaudí based his designs on the complex forms we know today as helicoids, hyperboloids and hyperbolic paraboloids. These are forms abstracted from nature and were translated into the design of the columns, vaults and intersecting geometric elements of the structure of the Sagrada Família. Look up at the vault crowning the interior of the basilica's nave. Does this resemble a dense forest of trees with sunlight shining through it? Everything he designed, declared Gaudi, came from the 'Great Book of Nature'; his 'textbooks' were the mountains and caves he loved to explore.

In fact, when Mark Burry, a 23-year-old New Zealander came to Barcelona in 1980, and became involved in trying to piece the fragments of Gaudí's remaining architectural models of the Sagrada Família together, he was unable to make sense of their unfamiliar and demanding geometry until the peseta dropped and he realized the relation of Gaudí's mathematical imagination to the rock formations of mountains, among other natural phenomena. Burry went on to become both the executive architect of the Sagrada Família and a leading light in spatial design and computer programming at RMIT University, Melbourne. Devising parametric computer-modelling techniques, adapted from the aerospace industry, he has been able to complete Gaudí's designs. Working under Jordi Faulí i Oller, director of works in Barcelona, he has even sped up the construction process by having stones cut by computer-driven machinery.

During the Spanish Civil War, Catalan anarchists destroyed what few models and sketches there were by Gaudí's hand. They did, however, leave the architect's tomb intact. For, whatever their grudge against General Franco and the Catholic Church, they knew full well that the architect was considered a saint by people of all classes and political beliefs – indeed, today, the Association for the Beatification of Antoni Gaudí campaigns for the architect to be officially declared a saint.

It may be difficult for puritan eyes to look at, and yet this brilliant feat of imaginative construction has inspired designs by some of the world's finest engineers and architects over the past century, Oscar Niemeyer, Frei Otto and Pier Luigi Nervi among them. It will continue to disturb the imaginations of generations to come, who may yet know its architect as San Antoni de Sagrada Família.

Looking heavenward to the elaborate vaults of the nave

Volkshalle by Albert Speer

A new Pantheon, or set design for Götterdämmerung?

According to Albert Speer, Hitler's ambitious architect and all-too-capable Minister of Armaments and War Production, the final performance by the Berlin Philharmonic before this distinguished orchestra abandoned Berlin in May 1945 opened with Brünnhilde's last aria – the vengeful valkyrie sings of setting fire to Valhalla – and the finale from Wagner's *Götterdämmerung*.

As the Russians neared Berlin that spring, Adolf Hitler continued to toy with plans, and a vast model, of Germania, the new German capital that was to be built over Berlin after the ultimate victory of the

Model of the unbuilt 'People's Hall', 1939

Third Reich. At the heart of this bombastic new city stood the colossal domed Volkshalle, a gigantic play on the ancient Roman Pantheon.

Speer had based his design on a sketch of the Roman temple made by Hitler himself in 1925, while in 1938 Hitler had made a point of visiting the Pantheon on an official trip to Rome. The Pantheon had been created for an empire that survived four centuries. The Volkshalle would go one better: it was to symbolize an empire planned to endure a thousand years. In the event, the Third Reich missed its target by 998 years, and neither the Volkshalle nor Germania were built.

With clever use of steel and lightweight concrete behind stone cladding, the Volkshalle would have been 290 metres (950 feet) high. The oculus, or roof light, in the centre of the dome would, at 46 metres (150 feet) in diameter, have been so big that Michelangelo's dome of St Peter's could have been lowered through it. In fact, 80 years on from the Fall of Berlin, it is still quite hard to understand just how enormous the Volkshalle would have been. So big inside, that when it was packed with triumphant, chanting Nazis, their breath would have caused condensation to form on the underside of the dome. This would have created clouds, and rain might well have fallen on the fervid crowds below – a suitably Wagnerian spectacle.

Curiously, when you stand back and study Speer's model of Germania, what it resembles least of all is a city of the future. It is not surprising that a leader who wished to be a new, if decidedly unholy, Roman Emperor should have been obsessed with Neoclassical design, nor is it odd that Hitler should have wanted to outdo his predecessors in terms of height, scale and ceremony.

And yet, what the imperious Volkshalle resembles most is an enormous funerary monument. Above its mighty portico, Speer should have had this esoteric legend inscribed: *Et in Arcadia Ego* (I [Death] am in Arcadia, too). Arcadia means utopia, and utopia means nowhere. The Third Reich was headed nowhere. As Hitler and his pet architect played with the design of the Volkshalle, Berlin and the Third Reich were about to be engulfed in flames, just as Valhalla – home of all the Nordic gods – was in Wagner's *Götterdämmmerung*. The Volkshalle proved to be less than a pantheon to a master race of black-clad German demigods, and more a tomb in the cemetery of Hitler and Speer's over-excited imaginations.

Eiffel Tower
Engineering masterpiece
or aesthetic blunder?

On Valentine's Day 1887, the French newspaper *Le Temps* published a love letter of sorts to Paris by the self-styled 'Committee of Three Hundred'. It took the form of an attack on Gustave Eiffel's radical 300-metre- (980-feet-) high wrought iron tower, newly under construction in the city's Champ de Mars. It was signed by such grand establishment arts figures as the writer Guy de Maupassant, Charles Gounod, composer of the opera *Roméo et Juliette*, and that industrious painter of waxen nude ladies, William-Adolphe Bouguereau.

'We, writers, painters, sculptors, architects and passionate devotees of the hitherto untouched beauty of Paris', thundered the three hundred, 'protest with all our strength, with all our indignation in the name of slighted French taste, against the erection ... of this useless and monstrous Eiffel Tower.'

The French engineer's soaring achievement was nothing more than a 'hateful column of bolted sheet metal' to these men of late nineteenth-century high taste. When completed in 1889 – it was the gateway for the highly successful Paris World's Fair of that year – friends of Maupassant said he came either to picnic under the tower or else to dine in one of its restaurants every day, as these were the only places from where he could not see the monstrosity.

Far from being useless, as the 'Three Hundred' asserted, the Eiffel Tower became an important communications mast in an era when Maupassant's stories would be read over the new-fangled wireless and even turned, not so many years later, into television plays broadcast via, yes, Eiffel's 'hateful column'. More than this, though, in the early days of World War I, a radio transmitter located in the tower jammed German wireless communications, helping to save Paris from invasion. Might Maupassant, who had fought as a soldier in the Franco-Prussian War of 1870–71, have changed his tune then?

Sketch by engineer Maurice Koechlin, 1884

(1)

Pylône de 300 m de hauteur
pour la ville de Paris 1889.
Avant Projet de M. E. Nouguier et M. Koechlin

Paris le 6 juin 1884.

Echelle 1/50

Perhaps, but the writer died young in 1893, taking nineteenth-century attitudes concerning what was and what was not art to his grave in the Cimetière de Montparnasse. This city graveyard is overlooked by the vertiginous bulk of Tour Montparnasse, an unforgiving skyscraper completed in 1973. It drew such negative criticism that, from then on, no new building over seven storeys was to be tolerated in the city centre. This, at least, was something for late twentieth-century Maupassants to write home about.

As for Eiffel's tower, it went on not just to be useful, but to be admired and even loved. To date, more than 250 million people have ascended the 'hateful column' by lift or stairs, while in an era of High-Tech architecture and spectacular structural engineering, its design and construction seem all the more wondrous. Positions of the two-and-a-half-million rivet holes in the 7,500 tonnes of ironwork were specified to within 0.1 mm, and this at a time when components arrived at a construction site by horse and cart.

When Eiffel spoke to journalists about the way the tower would look he said, 'Do not the laws of natural forces always conform to the secret laws of harmony?' However, when the engineer first saw the initial proposal for the tower that was to bear his name depicting a 'great pylon, consisting of four lattice girders standing apart at the base and coming together at the top, joined together by metal trusses at regular intervals', drawn by 28-year-old Maurice Koechlin, one of his assistants, he was concerned with its artless appearance. Eiffel asked Stephen Sauvestre, his company architect, to make the design more palatable to Parisian taste. Sauvestre added decorative arches around the base and various other frills that dressed the tower as if for a genteel promenade along the Champ de Mars.

Designed for a life of 20 years, the long-lived tower has become as much a part of Paris as Maupassant's adored Notre-Dame. It acts as a landmark, a point of orientation, and a communications mast, while every evening it lights up in a blaze of flashing coloured lights, exhibiting a frivolous side to its otherwise stern character. To many cultured Parisians in 1889 the Eiffel Tower was an aesthetic blunder. A century before Maupassant's damning letter to the press, some of his fellow countryman were attacking the gloom and barbarity of medieval Gothic cathedrals like Notre-Dame. Today, we can enjoy both, and even read a Maupassant short story while looking up at the tower he and his Committee of Three Hundred so despised.

Casa del Fascio/Casa del Popolo
Classical or Modern? Totalitarian or democratic?

The change of name says so much about this profound and pivotal twentieth-century Italian building. Designed by Giuseppe Terragni and built between 1932 and 1936 alongside Como Cathedral, it was one of many such community halls and headquarters for local Italian fascist parties erected during the 20-year dictatorship of Benito Mussolini. It was, though, by far the finest.

After Mussolini had been shot and strung up from a lamppost in Milan, Terragni's Casa del Fascio went quietly back to work in a democratic world as the Casa del Popolo. Its serene architecture, at once classical and modern, had no issues with a new political and social order that its architect, a fervent fascist, would have found abhorrent and effete.

Casa del Fascio celebrating the common goals of Nazi Germany and Fascist Italy

The Casa del Fascio raises important questions. Just how political are the forms and lineaments of architecture? Has there ever been such a thing as fascist or democratic architecture? Do we associate Nazi architecture with serried ranks of classical columns, mighty domes and vast parade-ground squares? Perhaps we do, and yet the very same architecture frames and defines the democracy of the United States of America.

And who, today, walking past Ernst Sagebiel's former Aviation Ministry in Berlin associates this impressive public office with the evils of Nazism? It was, after all, built as Hermann Goering's headquarters and was intended to be a symbol of Nazi strength. But, for most people, it is no more or less Nazi than the Shell Centre (1961) – a corporate headquarters crowned with a 26-storey tower in central London – designed by Howard Robertson, an American-born architect who had fought the Germans on the front line in World War I. He had been promoted to colonel and won the Military Cross as well as the Legion d'honneur. Robertson, who was elected President of the Royal Institute of British Architects, was a democrat through and through, and yet, if the Germans had won World War II, the Nazis might well have commissioned a headquarters very much like the Shell Centre.

Planned as a perfect square rising half as high as its width, the Casa del Fascio encloses a courtyard designed for parades and public gatherings. Although its geometry is relentless, the building is complex. Each facade is different, and the interior fits together, as many writers have observed, like some giant Rubik's Cube. Clad in white marble, this concrete-and-glass building – at once transparent and enclosed – has the feel of a classical temple or Renaissance palazzo seen through a twentieth-century lens. It is, quite simply, one of the great buildings of all time.

As for Giuseppe Terragni, he died at the age of 39 in July 1943, just weeks before Italy surrendered to the Allies. He was never to know how his Casa del Fascio would live on with a different name and in a wholly different world and yet be admired and cherished, perhaps even more than it had been in the 1930s.

Guggenheim Bilbao
Iconic folly or inspired urban sculpture?

The inauguration of the truly spectacular Guggenheim Museum, Bilbao, was every bit as dramatic as the building itself. On 17 October 1997, the day before King Juan Carlos I was to have declared the museum open, a plot by Basque ETA terrorists to kill him was uncovered. Three terrorists dressed as gardeners had tried to place bombs in flowerpots around Jeff Koons's playful *Puppy* sculpture, sited close to the museum's entrance, where the Spanish king would have addressed the crowds gathered for the occasion. A Basque police officer, José María Aguirre, foiled the plot, but was shot dead by the pretend gardeners.

Frank Gehry's museum certainly had an explosive impact on Bilbao, and on contemporary architecture and urban planning, too. Looking like nothing else, its sculptural folds of curving titanium caught and refracted daylight while, intellectually and emotionally, dazzling visitors, critics and politicians from around the world. A wayward, beautiful thing, it rises from redundant Bilbao dockyards and so, unlike, for example, the dim-witted 2015 design for a branch

Guggenheim Museum, Bilbao, viewed from the Nervión River

of the Guggenheims set slap in the middle of Helsinki's city centre, Gehry's tour de force breathed new life into a largely forgotten part of Bilbao, animating its skyline and, in the process, drawing 4 million visitors to the city between 1997 and 2000. The Basque government claimed that the revenue earned from the 4 million paid for the construction of the building.

Popular with visitors, it wowed most critics and set the minds of all too many city politicians racing. What if the 'Bilbao Effect', as it came to be known, could be repeated elsewhere? The visitors, the revenue, the acclaim and awards for politicians! This, more or less, is exactly what happened. Around the world, cities began to vie for the most outlandish, wilful or 'iconic' buildings. Within a decade, not just museums and art galleries, but office blocks and even town halls sprouted whimsically in a global city play-garden.

The problem, as with the work of Le Corbusier and Mies van der Rohe, is that not every architect who would like to be as creative as Frank Gehry *is* as creative as Frank Gehry. Nor does every major city centre need a building as happily wild as the Guggenheim Bilbao. The commissioning of buildings and urban planning are arts as well as financial deals and imperfect sciences. Bilbao happened to get it right. All too many other cities got it wrong, with perversely wayward buildings mocking both science and art.

Churlish and opportunistic critics took this as an opportunity to attack Frank Gehry, as if this maverick Canadian-American architect had wittingly unleashed clown-like architecture around the globe. By 2015, a reaction to 'iconic' architecture had become the critical norm. Gehry meanwhile, an architect-artist, continued to delight and infuriate in equal measure, as did the Bilbao Guggenheim, but this is also one of the undoubted architectural wonders of the twentieth century.

Puppy, by Jeff Koons, in front of the museum

Bauhaus, Dessau
Vision of a Modern paradise or functionalist purgatory?

Founded in Dessau in 1919 by Walter Gropius, the Bauhaus was an all-inclusive school of art, design, craft and, ultimately, architecture, its purpose to mesh artistic and design skills with the needs of industry. Designed by Gropius and completed in 1925, the school's purpose-built home was a model of Industrial Functionalism, a refined and elegant factory encapsulating its core beliefs.

From this crisp new building, the Bauhaus spread its message across Continental Europe, inspiring a new generation of young architects. And yet, Gropius's ideas did not always fall on fertile ground. It was in England that the Bauhaus was most questioned, and even ridiculed. The leading English architectural journal of the late 1920s – the *Architectural Review*, directed by the insightful young publisher Hubert de Cronin Hastings – employed an array of writers, including Philip Morton Shand, an erudite and well-travelled sophisticate who introduced its readers to the latest developments on

The Staatliches-Bauhaus (Building House), Dessau

Gropius's office at the Bauhaus

the Continent. At the same time, Hastings employed the mercurial young John Betjeman – the future poet laureate – among whose first pieces for the *AR* was an essay entitled 'The Death of Modernism', published well before most British architects had thought much about the Bauhaus.

Betjeman's friend, Evelyn Waugh, published his first novel, *Decline and Fall*, in 1928, a year after the first English translation of Le Corbusier's epochal *Vers une architecture* (*Towards a New Architecture*, see page 81). In this bitingly funny novel, readers were introduced to Professor Otto Silenus, a humourless young German architect commissioned on a whim to build a new Bauhaus-style country house by a fashionable socialite. 'The problem of architecture as I see it', he tells a visiting journalist, 'is the problem of all art – the elimination of the human element from the consideration of form. The only perfect building must be the factory, because that is built to house machines, not men.'

Despite this singularly English attack, there were real criticisms to be made of the German design factory. Women could study and practise weaving and decorative arts, but not architecture. Gropius saw this as a specifically male calling. And the Bauhaus building, as with so many of those it inspired, proved to be cold in winter, hot in summer and in need of more maintenance than its nominally 'functional' design would suggest. There was, then, a justified suspicion on the part of those wary of 'Modernism' that the Bauhaus was more about appearance than true functionalist architecture and design.

Curiously, when the English and their fellow Britons chose to go Modern – essentially after World War II – they did so with a brutal rigour that surprised even Walter Gropius. By this time, the founder of the Bauhaus was in the United States, where he designed buildings that were not a patch on the Bauhaus School itself. In the 1960s he made a foray into English architecture, designing, of all projects, the Playboy Club for Hugh Hefner in Mayfair. Here was a building given over, perhaps a little too closely, to the human element, and especially its subservient female form.

Chapel of the Holy Shroud, Turin
Religious or architectural miracle?

For structural bravura and sheer spine-tingling mystery, the walk between the choir of Turin Cathedral in northern Italy, and the circular Chapel of the Holy Shroud secreted behind and beyond it, is hard to beat. Anyone with the slightest interest in architectural originality should make this pilgrimage at least once in their lives.

Whatever you believe about the Holy Shroud – the linen cloth inexplicably imprinted with an image of a man that has haunted devout Christians, avowed sceptics, scientists, artists and conspiracy theorists for many hundreds of years – the chapel designed to house this haunting relic is, without doubt, miraculous. Tragically, it was badly damaged by fire in 1997 and, in 2015, it was still *chiuso per restauro* (closed for restoration).

From the apse of Turin Cathedral, visitors climbed a bible-black marble stair, emerging into the confines of the chapel, it too sheathed in funereal, although lustrous, black marble. At the chapel's core was a black-and-gold altar, a Baroque exuberance designed by the architect and engineer Antonio Bertola. Towards its encrusted peak a glass

Spire rising above the dome of the Chapel of the Holy Shroud, Turin

case displayed and protected the mysterious shroud. The true wonder here, however – the overwhelming surprise – was the diffused daylight coursing down from interstices of the astonishing dome centred over the altar, defining the dimensions of this cosseting place of reverence and bewilderment.

Constructed between 1688 and 1694, the Chapel of the Holy Shroud is the inexhaustible masterpiece of Camillo-Guarino Guarini (1624–83), a Theatine priest – a member, that is, of a Counter-Reformation Roman Catholic order – and one of the most intensely original of Italy's celebrated Baroque architects. Soaring in intersecting tiers of stone geometry above the altar, this compelling, confounding structure was designed to celebrate and deepen the mystery of the shroud and – perhaps inevitably – to champion Guarini's patron and the relic's guardian, Charles Emmanuel II, of the royal House of Savoy.

Not that Guarini's ambitious client was as holy as his family's famous relic, or in any way as numinous in his dealings as his architect was in his designs. Only 13 years before construction of the chapel began, Charles Emmanuel had ordered a massacre of local Protestants, who had proved resistant to a choice between attending Catholic Mass or a forced removal to remote mountain valleys. The killings were singularly brutal; enough to prompt John Milton,

Looking up into the interlocking sorcery of Guarini's dome

hundreds of miles away in England, to write a sonnet bemoaning their fate.

Even so, the appeal of Guarini's chapel and mesmeric dome has survived every doubt about the House of the Savoy and the mysterious linen cloth in its stewardship. The confidence of the design is rooted, perhaps, not simply in Guarino's undoubted artistry, but in his geocentric view of the universe – the Earth at the centre of divine creation – and his mastery of mathematics. He wrote four books on the subjects, one of which, *Euclides adauctus* ('Euclides Expanded'), is an early treatise on descriptive geometry, or how to represent three-dimensional objects and spaces in two dimensions. It was this skill that allowed Guarini to realize his dome with such imagination and geometric precision: even with today's computer programs, its structure would take some time to model.

Several years before he began work on the chapel, Guarini spent time in Spain, where he studied Moorish architecture. Look up again at his dome, and the laced geometry of the Great Mosque of Córdoba is evident in its rich play of overlapping and receding structural elements. In Rome, too, Guarini would have visited the intense, voluptuous and architecturally demanding churches of the earlier Baroque architect Francesco Borromini. And yet, there is something more than these influences – and the domineering aspirations of his Torinese clients – informing the design. That something is, of course, the shroud itself, an object that for this brilliant Theatine priest was – to borrow Winston Churchill's famous description of the Soviet Union – 'a riddle, wrapped in a mystery, inside an enigma'. Guarini's genius was to compound this sacred puzzle by shrouding it with a dome of unparalleled sophistication and religious mystery.

Guarini's tour de force demonstrates how a sense of ineffable mystery can be represented in three solid dimensions, a solidity pierced and toyed with by daylight, making darkness visible and light feel almost tangible. The Chapel of the Holy Shroud remains a pinnacle of the arts of architecture and mathematics in the service of an idea as hard to believe as Guarini's dumbfounding design. The miracle here is as much in Guarini's profound *coup de théâtre* as in the enigmatic relic it cocoons.

Deconstructivism
Architecture meets philosophy or fashion?

'Architecture aims at Eternity', wrote Sir Christopher Wren, 'and therefore, is the only thing incapable of modes and fashions in its principles.' Imagine telling this to the Deconstructivists, a loose-knit and spiky cluster of international architects who, at the tail end of the twentieth century and into the twenty-first, appeared to do their disconcerting best to undermine and overthrow age-old canons of architectural logic, propriety, taste and structure.

Nominally, at least, their guiding star was Jacques Derrida (1930–2004), the Algerian-born French philosopher whose many

Bernard Tschumi's folie in Parc de la Villette, Paris

writings on semiotics set out to challenge and deconstruct no less than the dominant discourse of Western culture. While this was a perfectly valid philosophical enquiry – the kind discussed with shrugged shoulders and artful looks over *pastis* at corner cafes in Paris – it translated awkwardly into architecture.

A riposte to Postmodernism (see page 115), Deconstructivism nurtured wilfully fragmented, visually disconcerting buildings, the forms of which bordered on the chaotic. The style made its debut in Paris in 1982 with the Parc de la Villette design competition. This was won by Bernard Tschumi with a design for a park in the city's 19th arrondissement, of fragmented monuments, mostly bright red, that you can walk around today. Tschumi had held long conversations with Derrida.

Ever alert to new fashions in architecture, in 1988 Philip Johnson curated a 'Deconstructivist Architecture' exhibition with Mark Wigley, architect and academic, at New York's Museum of Modern Art. This showed the works of seven iconoclastic contemporary architects – Frank Gehry, Zaha Hadid, Rem Koolhaas, Coop Himmelb(l)au, Daniel Libeskind, Peter Eisenman and Bernard Tschumi – although only Eisenman and Tschumi linked their oeuvre specifically to Derrida and Deconstructivism itself.

In the early built work of Daniel Libeskind – notably his Jewish Museum, Berlin (2001) – the fragmentation of ideas posited by Derrida achieved a certain profundity. The museum's very structure, along with its shattered plan, evoked the savage break-up and destruction of the city's Jewish population in the 1930s and '40s. In reality, though, the work of architects like Libeskind, Hadid and Gehry was individualistic, owing more to imagination and practical concerns than to French semiotics. While buildings as disparate as Frank Gehry's Vitra Design Museum at Weil am Rhein, Germany (1989), and Rem Koolhaas's Seattle Central Library (2004) have been labelled Deconstructivist, this has little meaning beyond what it says about this catch-all tag.

As with Postmodernism, Deconstructivism became a fashion leading to a spate of wacky buildings around the world – with no clear or rational end in sight by 2015 – where fashionable forms followed computer programs rather than French philosophy.

Palácio da Alvorada, Brasília

Bauhaus in Brazil, or Brazil into Bauhaus?

In 1936, Oscar Niemeyer (1907–2012), a young Brazilian architect, was sent to meet Le Corbusier, the greatest living Modern architect, when he arrived in Rio de Janeiro on board the *Graf Zeppelin*, the transatlantic German airship. Corbu descended from the air, Niemeyer told me, like 'a mighty god visiting his pygmy worshippers. We were, of course, in awe of him. We knew we should know all about Walter Gropius and the Bauhaus, too, but we saw something other than machine worship and a rigidly European manner in Le Corbusier.'

While Le Corbusier learned much from the sensual dance of Brazilian forms, it was Niemeyer, although he learned from Le Corbusier, who went on to make these his brilliant trademark. Commissioned, with Lúcio Costa, to design Brasília, the long-promised new Brazilian capital city, Niemeyer's first monumental building there was the diaphanous Palácio da Alvorada (1958), the official residence of the president of Brazil. Breathtakingly beautiful, the palace shimmers on a peninsula, all perfectly clipped, emerald-green grass and hummingbirds, overlooking Lake Paranoá, a waterway created as part of the design of the new city, so very far from Rio and the sea.

'What is Brasília', said the dynamic president, Juscelino Kubitschek, who willed the new capital into being within just four years, 'if not the dawn [*alvorada*] of a new day for Brazil?' A new dawn for Modern architecture, too. Here, the rationalism of Modern design meets the colours, the visual dance, the sheer vibrancy of Brazilian art and culture. Here, Modern art is hung alongside historic tapestries, and the Baroque meets the Bauhaus. Chippendale chairs from eighteenth-century England vie discreetly for attention with Barcelona chairs by Mies van der Rohe. Dappled light reflected from the lake ripples gently across rich marble floors and plain white ceilings. The effect of this marriage of modern and historic art and design, of rational and sensuous architecture is utterly captivating.

Although the Palácio de Alvorada has certain roots in German Modernism – Niemeyer, as his name suggests, was of part German descent – this mellifluous building is also a very long way indeed, whether geographically, culturally or by airship, from Dessau and the Bauhaus.

'I have always wanted my buildings to be as light as possible', Niemeyer told me, 'to touch the ground gently, to swoop and soar, and to surprise. Architecture is invention. It must offer pleasure as well as practicality. If you only worry about function, the result stinks. Many of my buildings have been political and civic monuments, but perhaps some of them have also given ordinary people, powerless people, a sense of delight.'

Oscar Niemeyer told me another story. 'Walter Gropius came to see me at my house at Canoas above Rio. I designed it in a sequence of natural curves to flow in and out of the existing landscape. He said, "it's beautiful, but it can't be mass-produced". As if I had intended such a thing! What an idiot.'

South facade of the Palácio de Alvorada overlooking Niemeyer's reflecting pool

Crystal Palace

One-year wonder, or one of history's most influential buildings?

Within three weeks of the announcement of the Great Exhibition in 1850, a distinguished committee chaired by the civil engineer William Cubitt and including Robert Stephenson, Isambard Kingdom Brunel and Charles Barry, co-architect of the new Palace of Westminster, had received 253 entries from around the world for the design of a building to house the very first World's Fair, or Expo, in central London. The committee rejected the lot.

With the May 1851 deadline looming, and with no obvious solution in sight, Joseph Paxton, a gardener and greenhouse designer, decided to have a go. His first sketch – pen on pink blotting paper, drawn on a train and happily preserved – was a stroke of genius. What Paxton proposed was a vast, pre-assembled building – 563 metres (1,848 feet) long – its cast-iron and plate-glass components mass-produced, transported as efficiently as possibly to Hyde Park and pieced together using the quickest and latest methods available.

Plate glass was new at the time, yet Paxton based the entire strategy of his 'Crystal Palace' on this new material. Not only would the giant exhibition hall be light and easy to assemble, but all those thousands of panes of glass would create a bright interior with little need for artificial lighting. Heat was to be controlled with louvres and canvas rolled over the glass at critical points on summer days.

Paxton's masterpiece was, to say the least, a brilliant success. Its huge, column-free spaces allowed exhibition designers the free flow of their imaginations, while the 6 million people – a third of Britain's population at the time – who came to gawp at the wonders of global art and trade, and even to 'spend a penny' in the flushing public lavatories installed inside the building, were clearly in awe of all they saw. So, when the Great Exhibition ended that October, a decision was made to take the building down and to reassemble it in southeast London. And, while doing so, to make it even bigger.

And so, although the Crystal Palace appeared to have come and gone in central London in little more than one intense instant, it lived on as a hugely popular venue for every conceivable form of entertainment – from highbrow to lowbrow – until one fateful night in 1936 when, for whatever reason, it caught fire, imploded and vanished in a very big puff of smoke.

But was that the end of the Crystal Palace? No. Not only had Paxton's building won public admiration, its design was acclaimed by architects, engineers and contractors. It had been much cheaper to build than rival designs proposed in conventional materials, and it had been constructed and assembled in record time. More than this, it showed how truly flexible, indeterminate interior space could be shaped inside a building; inside such a building, anything could go: warehouse, office, factory … railway station, airport, shopping mall, Lloyd's of London. And all these uses came to pass, notably from the 1970s, in diverse and enduring buildings that looked, self-consciously or otherwise, to Paxton's Crystal Palace for their inspiration.

Colour illustration of the interior during the Great Exhibition, 1851

Centre Pompidou, Paris
Oil refinery or refined public gallery?

The Pompidou Centre (1977), designed by a team led by the architects Renzo Piano and Richard Rogers and the structural engineer Peter Rice, is one of the most striking, monumental twentieth-century city-centre buildings.

As Joseph Paxton had been with the Crystal Palace in 1850, the winners of the competition for its design – young, bearded and long-haired – were outsiders, and their proposal outlandish. What Piano, Rogers and Rice had come up with was a huge, Crystal Palace-like shed, forged from iron, concrete and glass, providing vast open-plan interiors in which anything might happen in an era of art-world 'happenings'. Rogers himself likened it to 'a cross between the British Museum and Times Square'. It was as hip a design for a public building as could be imagined, a cultural centre for the iconoclastic new worlds of Pierre Boulez in music, Andy Warhol in art and Jean-Luc Godard on screen.

Visitors – and there were to be 6 million of them each year, five times more than expected – would go up and down to the centre's

Exterior seen from the public square, with glass escalator tubes

various levels by escalators in glazed tubes on the outside of the building. This kept space clear inside, gave visitors animated views of central Paris and enlivened the facade of this spectacular blue, red and white structure.

Here was a great machine of a building, winking and grinning at its polite, low-rise neighbours. It seems remarkable that it was ever commissioned, especially during the era of the right-wing Gaullist French president, Georges Pompidou, after whom the Centre is named.

So very familiar today, in the 1970s the Pompidou Centre was a bitterly controversial project. Unlike the Crystal Palace, it was not going to go away. Its construction involved the sweeping away of the hugely popular Les Halles food markets – the 'belly of Paris' – while its appearance was, inevitably, likened to that of an oil refinery. When Richard Rogers admitted to an elderly Parisian lady that he was one of the architects, she set about him with her umbrella.

When the patrician Georges Pompidou was shown the design, he gave a Gallic shrug, saying no more than *Ca va faire crier* ('This is going to make a noise'). It did. Noisier, perhaps, than an oil refinery in full swing. Now, though, it is hard to remember Paris pre-Centre Pompidou.

Colourful ducts and pipes on the characteristic exterior

Säynätsalo Town Hall, Finland
Convincing new vernacular, or precursor of vernacular kitsch?

Säynätsalo Town Hall rises in layers of beautifully laid, soft orange-red bricks from a forum-like site in the heart of an island on Lake Paijanne. Opened in 1952, it is one of the best works of the Finnish architect Alvar Aalto. Designed to house not only this small community's town hall, but also shops, flats and a library, this pitch-perfect building animates its forest setting while blending into it. By any standards, this is twentieth-century Modernism with a heart, soul and sense of place.

Grass-covered stairs to the internal courtyard

Unpretentiously, it marries the ideals of an Italian Renaissance palazzo, a Roman forum (or Greek agora) and distinctly Modern design with nature. Processional steps leading up to the entrance of the council chamber area are fashioned from local timber overlain with grass. The council chamber itself – white and light – is crowned with a timber roof paying gentle homage to those of medieval European town halls. The bricks of external walls are laid in a slightly wavy fashion to give the building a handcrafted feel and emotional warmth.

So, surely, there is nothing one can possibly say against this enchanting Finnish building, at once rational, functional, emotionally intelligent and in tune with its rural setting. Well, not exactly. The one problem with Säynätsalo is that, through no fault of its own, it nurtured countless thousands of dismal, bricky 'vernacular' buildings, especially town halls, across Europe in the 1970s and 1980s.

These earnest buildings were an understandable reaction on the part of equally earnest and well-meaning architects to get away from what they, and a great part of the public, saw as cold, hard and even brutally Modern buildings lacking craft and soul. And yet, a pitched roof or two, brick walls and timber window frames are not the same thing as a true vernacular design, much less convincing architecture.

This derivative 'neo-vernacular' style was short-lived. Real vernacular design comes from an understanding of place. It is not a style as such, but a way of seeing, thinking and feeling, connecting buildings to local cultures and histories as well as landscapes and materials. At Säynätsalo, a small paper-industry town remote from Helsinki, Alvar Aalto showed how a modern vernacular architecture could be shaped in the most convincing manner.

Carcassone

Medieval Europe revisited, or the seeds of Disneyland sown?

From across the vine-rich fields and craggy prominences of Languedoc-Roussillon, Carcassone looks every inch the perfect walled medieval city. Its turrets, towers and embattlements evoke a world of chivalrous, jousting knights, courtly damsels and military valour in God's service. Here, if anywhere, a king might have held court in a chamber dominated by a round table and spoken of the quest for the Holy Grail, a device that first appeared in *Perceval, le conte du Graal* (*Perceval: The Story of the Grail*), an unfinished early twelfth-century French romance by Chrétien de Troyes.

Close up, and through its curiously perfect gateways, Carcassone proves to be a shrine to modern tourism, baseball caps replacing plumed helmets, T-shirts substituted for tabards and selfie-sticks in place of swords. No one should be accused of being cynical if, stepping this way, they think 'Is this medieval Languedoc or Disneyland?' It is a mistake commonly made.

A military stronghold since at least Roman times, Carcassone had fallen into such a state of disrepair by the mid-nineteenth century that in 1849 the French government issued a decree to demolish its once imposing medieval fortress, all but synonymous with the town. An uproar ensued. Later that year the architect and theorist Eugène Viollet-le-Duc was commissioned to restore it.

Viollet-le-Duc had very particular views about restoration. 'To restore an edifice', he wrote in *Dictionnaire raisonne*, 'is not to maintain it, repair or rebuild it, but to re-establish it in a complete state that may never have existed at a particular moment.' He had already restored Notre-Dame in Paris, adding what details – and gargoyles – he took a fancy to. At Carcassone, Viollet-le-Duc courted controversy by demolishing ancient buildings he thought unworthy of his grand project and using building materials shipped in from elsewhere in France.

This made the French Gothic Revivalist something of a bogeyman to conservationists in other countries, and notably so in

England where the eminent Victorian critic John Ruskin campaigned for the gentle and authentic restoration of historic buildings. Ruskin's banner was carried forward by the designer, poet and political activist William Morris, who founded the Society for the Protection of Ancient Buildings based on the principle of what he called 'anti-scrape'. In other words, on no account should the patina, accumulated over centuries, be scraped from venerable buildings.

This was poppycock to Viollet-le-Duc, which is why Carcassone has the appearance of a very well-made nineteenth-century stage set rather than that of a restored fortified medieval town. Even today, French conservationists (see Chartres Cathedral, page 24) have a tendency to follow in the heavy footsteps of Viollet-le-Duc, despite the adoption, more or less worldwide, of 'anti-scrape'. Carcassone does indeed have a Disneyland air about it. Walt Disney and his associates adored the look of the restored town. And yet, looking back across those vineyards and Cathar-haunted hills, how glorious Carcassone appears to be.

Carcassone, against the equally dramatic backdrop of the Black Mountain

Russian Revolutionary Architecture
Revolution for communism or capitalism?

Has architecture ever been truly revolutionary? For the most part, the story of architecture is a continuum, with occasional bumps and jolts. And yet, there was one brief period in modern history when architecture and revolution truly marched hand in hand. Although the leaders of the Bolshevik Revolution, who in 1917 overthrew centuries of Tsarist rule, were largely indifferent to the latest moves in art and architecture, their advocacy of a new kind of classless society encouraged a generation of architects who had been toying with radical new ideas from before World War I to let rip with a torrent of revolutionary ideas.

Konstantin Melnikov's Workers Club, Moscow

It was as if a bolt of electricity had shot through the currents of early twentieth-century architecture. In those few years, the invention of Russian architects was extraordinary. There was Vladimir Tatlin's proposal for a 400-metre- (1,310-foot-) high Monument to the Third International (an organization dedicated to world communism), a red steel tower, spiralling upwards around a tilted central axis around which glass chambers were to have rotated. There was the Narkomfin building in Moscow, by Moisei Ginzburg and Ignaty Milinis, an enormous block of concrete flats predating Le Corbusier's Unité d'Habitation, Marseilles, by two decades; given over to 'socialist' living, with communal kitchens and laundries, the Narkomfin's aim was to liberate women from domestic serfdom and everyone from capitalist domination. There were workers' clubs in radical new buildings. The most famous of these, by Konstantin Melnikov in Moscow, featured cantilevered concrete floors jutting out at angles. And, there was Vladimir Shukhov's 160-metre- (525-foot-) high broadcasting tower, coursing up above the Moscow skyline in a hyperboloid steel gridshell.

Such thrilling designs inspired the concrete megastructures of 1960s Europe, the High-Tech architecture that emerged in the 1970s, and the work of individual architects like James Stirling and James Gowan, Daniel Libeskind, Rem Koolhaas and, especially, Zaha Hadid, an ardent admirer of the Constructivist architecture movements that gave rise to this burst of radical creativity from the time of World War I.

It was to be short lived. Joseph Stalin took against Modern design in the 1930s. Architects, artists and designers who appeared not to toe the Stalinist line were purged alongside politicians, soldiers and intellectuals. Today, many of the buildings that have survived purges, war, and social and political upheavals in Russia are in a poor state of repair. They represent a culture very different indeed from the ideals of the modern Russian state, where ultra-capitalism, rapacious property development and crude design rule the roost.

In a fascinating twist of history, however, Russian revolutionary architecture has lived on in the capitalist West. Those few years of unbridled creativity have served as a treasure chest of images and ideas that architects outside Russia have plundered for decades. How curious, how ironic it would have seemed to Melnikov, Schukhov and Tatlin that Constructivism would serve capitalism better than it did the communism they so fervently believed would change the world, and architecture, for better and forever.

Mud
Glorious, or primitive building material?

In a world of steel, reinforced concrete and polymers, mud seems hopelessly out of place as a serious building material. Mud? This is surely no more than an oozy mess toyed with by children or wallowed in by pigs and hippopotamuses.

And yet, what a malleable, beautiful and enduring material mud can be. There are the deeply impressive mud mosques of Mali, in Djenné and Timbuktu, the former first constructed in 1325, and reconstructed in 1907. These mud-and-straw buildings are constantly renewed, lending them truly organic qualities, while, of course, they are wholly a part of the landscape and the very soil they rise from.

Mud has also been used to shape entire towns, like Bam in Iran, sadly devastated by a mighty earthquake in 2003, Ouarzazate in Morocco (an exotic location featured in a number of popular films, among them *Lawrence of Arabia*, *Gladiator* and *The Man Who Would Be King*) and Shibam, the 'Manhattan of the desert' in Yemen.

Djenné Mosque, Mali

For most visitors, a first sighting of Shibam across the desert is both puzzling and intoxicating. Here, clusters of tower houses – some 500 in all, dating from the sixteenth-century – rise up to 11-storeys, or 30 metres (100 feet), into a skyscape curtained with mountains. It is a magnificent sight, a mirage image of Manhattan.

Close up, however, many of the buildings appear to have been damaged by floods, terrorism – there was an Al-Qaeda attack on the town in 2009 – as well as through the use of domestic appliances like washing machines and modern plumbing that cause water to seep into the mud walls and undermine them.

Mud has proven to be a glorious material to build in, and has given us buildings of strange and wondrous beauty. By the chances of nature, the most ambitious mud buildings and cities are set in areas of the world most given to extremes of heat, to floods and earthquakes, along with violent religious and civil wars caused by destructive humans. Even then, the fairytale centre of Shibam has outlived those of all too many European and other advanced cities. Like the mosques of Mali, it remains an architectural and urban wonder.

The 'mud city' of Shibam, Yemen

Shreve, Lamb and Harmon

*Can you design one of the world's most
famous buildings and be forgotten?*

Completed in 1931, and for decades the tallest building in the world,
the 443-metre- (1,454-foot-) high Empire State Building remains *the*
landmark building of Manhattan, its story never less than dramatic.

Commissioned by John J. Raskob, a high-rolling New York
financier – and a papal knight and father of 13 children – who
worked for General Motors, the aim had been to outdo the new Art
Deco Chrysler Building on 42nd Street by going that bit higher than
this glamorously provocative rival. Raskob is said to have asked his
architect, 'How high can you make it so it won't fall down?'

But, although the 102-storey skyscraper, designed like an
elongated ziggurat, and clad in Indiana limestone, rocketed up from
Fifth Avenue at record speed, by the time President Herbert Hoover
declared it open, Wall Street had crashed and the United States was
plunged into the Great Depression. While the Hollywood movie *King
Kong* introduced the skyscraper to cinema audiences worldwide, few
firms moved into what became known as the 'Empty State Building'.

It took World War II to fill the tower with government offices,
and even then a USAAF B-25 Mitchell bomber did its best to bring
the building down when, on 28 July 1945, it crashed through swirling
fog into the National Catholic Welfare Council, housed on the 79th
and 80th floors, killing 14 people. It took another five years before
the Empire State Building turned a profit.

In 2001, after the shocking events of 11 September, when
terrorists led by Mohamed Atta, who had graduated in Egypt and
Germany as an architect and urban planner, flew into the twin towers
of the World Trade Center, destroying the Manhattan skyscrapers
and murdering almost 3,000, the Empire State Building became the
city's tallest building once again, In 2014, it was outgunned by the
541-metre (1,776-foot) One World Trade Center.

The brand new Empire State Building, towering over Manhattan

The charismatic Empire State Building has certainly led a dramatic life through momentous times, and yet remarkably few people – try asking on Fifth Avenue – can name its architect. The man who designed this world-famous skyscraper was William Lamb of Shreve, Lamb and Harmon, a firm founded in 1920 that produced one skyscraper after another over half a century, and yet remains as obscure as most of these buildings, none of them a patch on the Empire State Building.

Born in Brooklyn and trained at Columbia University and the École des Beaux-Arts, Paris, Lamb remains a shadowy figure in architectural history, his partners, skilled in planning and project direction, even more so. Especially in an era – the early twenty-first century – when personalities loom large in architecture, Lamb's near anonymity seems out of kilter with his very real achievement. But, Shreve, Lamb and Harmon, as with a number of the high-achieving US practices that followed in their quietly towering wake, were keen to be seen as business-like professionals rather than Renaissance artists. Still, when asked who designed the Empire State Building, it seems only right to answer without hesitation, William F. Lamb of Shreve, Lamb, and Harmon.

There is, though, something rather satisfying in the curious near anonymity of the Empire State Building. Although exceptionally tall, it fits comfortably into a streetscape lined with buildings few critics or historians can put a name to readily. Our need for authorship was nurtured from the Renaissance and has been compounded ever since by the rise of art history and scholarship. And, I suppose, by a kind of "I-Spy" mentality whereby we simply have to know who designed this or that building even when the evidence is cloudy.

From top: Richard H. Shreve, William F. Lamb and Charles B. Harmon

Stansted Airport
Ideal air terminal or banal shopping mall?

Opened in 1991, the new terminal at Stansted Airport, Essex, designed by Foster and Partners, was as revolutionary in terms of the airline industry as Frank Gehry's Guggenheim Bilbao (see page 41) was in the art world at the end of the same decade. Norman Foster, a skilled pilot, was keen to make the passenger experience as logical and as smooth as possible.

From the moment they entered the building, passengers would see a clear route to their departure gates and to the aircraft that would whisk them away on holiday. Stansted was to be as simple to use as the first civil airfields had been. In its High-Tech way, the new building would revive something of the glamour air travel had lost over the decades as terminals morphed into late twentieth-century representations of the nightmare visions of Hieronymus Bosch, although with none of the Dutch painter's artistry.

Foster's Stansted stood contemporary airport design on its head. All the machinery and services necessary to make a terminal work were buried in an undercroft, allowing the roof, designed with the

Interior when new, showing clear spaces and daylight filtering through the parasol roof

structural engineer Peter Rice, to be little more than a lightweight steel-and-glass parasol, or umbrella. Daylit for much of each day, the terminal was to be a far more pleasant and humane space than the low-ceilinged and harsh, fluorescent-lit corridors of all too many airports rushed up from the early 1960s.

Given that Stansted was devoted to low-cost, package-holiday flights, this was a significant and even altruistic move on the part of Foster's client, BAA (British Airports Authority). The former wartime US air force base had been transformed into one of the world's finest airports. But not for long ... Much to Foster's outrage, the graceful terminal was turned into a charmless souk. The British obsession with shopping meant that every available square foot of floor space was given over to a maze of garish shops. Aiming for Parnassus, Stansted's designers were brought down to land in the marketplace with a crude bump.

By the twenty-first century, most major airports – not just Stansted – had become gormless, edge-of-town shopping malls, with the sense that arrival and departure gates and aircraft had been added simply as an afterthought. And yet, the number of passengers passing through Stansted rose from a planned 8 million to 20 million a year, as ever more people expected cheap holidays in the sun as a right, and as romantic airliners became prosaic airbuses.

Clutter of kitsch shops obstructing passenger flow today

Taj Mahal

Great architecture or a greater story?

A love story in translucent white marble inlaid with precious stones, the Taj Mahal has long been one of the world's most enchanting buildings. Commissioned by Shah Jahan in 1632, this monumental domed tomb was built in memory of Mumtaz Mahal, the Mughal emperor's favourite wife, who died in childbirth.

The Persian architect Ustad Ahmad Lahauri was given a vast budget – as much as a billion US dollars today – a workforce of some 20,000, including most of the empire's skilled craftsmen, and 1,000 elephants to help transport material. With these, he shaped what was to become one of the world's most famous and best-loved buildings, its voluptuous dome rising between four sky-piercing minarets.

Defaced and stripped of some of its sumptuous decorative finery well before the fall of the Mughal Empire in the mid-nineteenth century, the building was restored by 1908 by order of Lord Curzon, Viceroy of India. Ever since, visitors have flocked to this tomb rising from sublime Persian gardens on the banks of the Yamuna River, although, astonishingly, an oil refinery was built close by, spitting acid rain at the white marble of the Taj Mahal. In recent years, restoration work has helped to conserve the building.

Miles away along the banks of the Yamuna, stands the Tomb of Humayun, an earlier Mughal emperor. Commissioned by Humayun's wife and designed by the Persian architect Mirak Mirza Ghiyas, built in Delhi between 1565 and 1572, this serene red sandstone structure crowned with a white marble dome has long been sidelined by the Taj Mahal. More severe in design than the tomb at Agra, it is, however, perhaps the more satisfying of these two Mughal tombs, from a strictly architectural point of view.

Where the undeniably beautiful Taj Mahal resembles a giant ornament, the Tomb of Humayun reads like a palatial urban building. Both have their virtues, yet I wonder if it is the compelling love story, played up for all it is worth by today's tourist industry, that has made the fairytale Taj Mahal by far the more famous.

The Taj Mahal reflected dreamily in the Yamuna River

San Carlo alle Quattro Fontane
Madness or masterpiece?

A wayward force of the High Renaissance, Baroque was broken in
by Michelangelo in Rome in the sixteenth century before being given
full rein by Bernini and Borromini in the seventeenth. Characterized
by curves, domes, broken pediments and a gloriously inventive
play on classical detailing, at its theatrical zenith it was thrilling
architectural opera – far from the chaste and graceful classicism that
both preceded it and ousted it in the eighteenth century. Deeply
romantic, it also had something of the subversive about it.

As did Francesco Borromini (1599–1667), architect of San Carlo
alle Quattro Fontane, a Roman church that retains the power to

Looking up into the complex geometry of Borromini's dome

provoke and thrill three-and-a-half centuries after its consecration. This was Borromini's first independent commission, received in 1634. He created a geometrically complex and serpentine building, writhing around an exquisite oval dome inside. From the street San Carlo presents an undulating facade, both concave and convex, as if stone was a plastic material to be moulded and sculpted at will.

Here is one of those buildings that is hard to sketch and difficult to understand. There are those who declare San Carlo nothing more than perverse kitsch, and Borromini mad. A passionate and troubled man, Borromini was to commit suicide, and yet, working with a single assistant and with nothing more than pen and paper, this seventeenth-century architect produced buildings that would challenge the most imaginative twenty-first-century architect armed with the latest computers, parametric theories and high-tech materials.

Born Francesco Castelli in Switzerland, the young stonemason worked on Milan Cathedral and St Peter's in Rome, newly crowned with Michelangelo's magnificent dome. He set up in practice in 1633 as one of the world's first professional architects under the pseudonym Borromini. For Borromini, architecture was truly a matter of life and death. While working in Rome on the rebuilding of the early Christian basilica, San Giovanni in Laterano, he discovered a man spitting on and disfiguring sacred stonework, and had the man beaten up. He died, and Borromini was granted a papal pardon. Studious, solitary, garbed in austere Spanish fashion, he lived in spartan rooms furnished with a library of more than 1,000 books, and a bust of Michelangelo.

Borromini was well aware of the challenging nature of his work. 'In inventing new things', he wrote, 'one cannot receive the fruit of one's labour except later.' Bernini said, after his rival's death, 'only Borromini understood this profession, but he was never content and wanted to hollow out one thing inside another, and another inside that without ever getting to the end.' Although his brilliance was recognized by German art historians from the 1920s, and later championed by English academics, even today there are lazily written guidebooks informing tourists that Borromini was insane. No. Borromini was inspired, a brilliant architect who played with complex forms and geometries to shape churches with passion and spirit. Few buildings are as restlessly alive and yet as serene as San Carlo alle Quattro Fontane.

Bibliothèque du Roi, Paris
Absolutist fantasy, or poetry from the French Enlightenment?

Étienne-Louis Boullée (1728–99) has left us just two fine, slightly idiosyncratic Parisian villas, nothing more. And yet, this Parisian architect had big dreams, visions of gigantic public buildings bigger than any built before the eighteenth century. In later centuries, only Albert Speer (see page 34), influenced by the French architect, would try to outdo him.

On first encounter, Boullée's schemes for the rebuilding of the King's Library, Paris, dating from 1785, might seem like the work of a megalomaniac, yet if there was any hint of madness in them, there was method, too. The idea of the Bibliothèque du Roi, with its Brobdingnagian reading room set under a coffered vault vanishing into a shadowy distance, was that of a home for *all* the world's books. Here, Parisians – not just the king – in an age of restless enquiry would have access to the ever-expanding sum of human knowledge. Although this project was drawn up during the heyday

Pen and ink sketch of the interior of King's Library by Boullée

of the French Enlightenment, it is hard to look at such drawings without equating them to ideas of absolutist power. But this is unfair hindsight, the shadow of twentieth-century totalitarianism falling over Boullée's drawing table, and not a true reflection of the architect's work or thought.

Boullée's was a world – and a political philosophy – apart from Joseph Stalin's Soviet Union. A design, however, for a Modernist palace of science and arts in Novosibirsk, the new Soviet capital of Siberia, was reworked by a team from Moscow led by A. Shoussev during World War II into an immense Neoclassical state opera house and theatre crowned with a giant dome resembling a design by, yes, Boullée, but seen through the distorting lens of the culture of a cruel and tyrannical state.

Boullée himself believed, above all, in the *poetry* of architecture. A brilliant draughtsman, he was a romantic whose work, despite its improbable scale, was ultimately – even if this is difficult to accept at first glance – humane.

Opera House, Novosibirsk, Siberia

Bibliothèque Nationale, Paris

*Folly on the Seine, or sane
new national library?*

What a strange way to stack and store the many millions of books of
France's most important public library. Not underground, nor shaded
in some top-lit Boullée-style stone hall, but in four high-rise glass towers,
rising from the corners of a windswept, rain-soaked, sun-baked podium
on the banks of the Seine.

Ah, but there is wit in the architecture here, *ne c'est pas?* The
towers have been shaped artfully in the guise of big books, folded at
their corners, their contents on display like the pages, yes, of big books.
How we laughed when the design of the Bibliothèque Nationale was
unveiled in the early 1990s.

Exterior showing the bookstack towers and steps

But 20 years on, this grand library has become a part of the Parisian cityscape. Open to all, covering all fields of knowledge, and sharing information with a network of European libraries, it is, in many ways, what Boullée had dreamed of. The design is by Dominique Perrault, a young architect when his appointment was announced in 1989. From the outset, and like other *Grands Projets* decreed by the socialist President François Mitterrand, the new library was intended to be a determinedly modern and striking monument.

Mitterrand had already courted controversy with the construction of a glass pyramid (1989), designed by the Chinese-American architect I. M. Pei, in the Cour Napoléon at the heart of the Louvre. If anything, Perrault's library sparked greater outrage, especially when its scale, lateness and cost overruns became something of a *cause célèbre*. The building was referred to sarcastically as the 'TGB' (Très Grande Bibliothèque), a play on the name of the French high-speed rail network, TGV (Train à Grande Vitesse), an even grander project, which had been a huge success.

When the library opened in 1996, detractors had a field day. Inside, Perrault had used precious wood from Brazilian rainforests, proving just how unsustainable this *folie de grandeur* was. And yet, for all the faults perceived 20 years ago, the TGB is a special place. It revived a semi-derelict quarter of Paris to the east of the Île de la Cité, while at the heart of its vast, elevated esplanade set between the four steel-and-glass book-end towers, and reached from the street by a truly monumental stair, is a great courtyard planted with 250 oaks, pines and birches. The building's lofty interiors are at once grand and intimate, with their thousands of quiet study spaces, crafted furniture and plays of daylight. As a functioning library, Perrault's *Grand Projet* is well into its stride, although its architecture will continue to divide opinion. There are those who find the library's esplanade too exposed, too slippery in winter, and others who find its design uncomfortably bleak. On a cold, grey Parisian day, its elemental exterior can seem too harsh, too remote from the streets around it, and altogether too much like a backdrop for some future remake of Jean-Luc Godard's *Alphaville*, a dystopian film that used the bleak new architecture of La Défense to haunting effect. Even then, the TGB has a certain modern drama about it, while on a sunny day, it is a pleasure to climb up and around it, to gawp – puzzled still, perhaps by those corner towers – and, of course, to settle down inside its fine interiors to read.

Le Corbusier
Hero or villain?

In 1907, Charles-Édouard Jeanneret, a 20-year-old architect and craftsman born and raised in Switzerland, travelled abroad for the first time. On the outskirts of Florence, he visited the Carthusian Charterhouse at Galluzo. Set on a hill and gathered around two Renaissance cloisters, it was a revelation. Here was *the* perfect way to live.

The long, deep cells of the monks, each with its own loggia, overlooked gardens, greenery and fresh air. The charterhouse offered privacy and community. Composed of many individual elements, it was nevertheless all of a piece.

Forty years later, the world-famous architect Le Corbusier would rework the Galluzo Charterhouse into a monumental concrete apartment block at Marseilles, overlooking gardens, sea, mountains and fresh air. This was the Unité d'Habitation (1952). In 1960, he would complete the Dominican monastery of Sainte Marie de la Tourette, 25 kilometres (15 miles) east of Lyon. Although made of the rawest concrete, and even wilfully ascetic, this monastic complex was also a case of Galluzo revisited.

Portrait of Le Corbusier by Nina Leen for Life *magazine, 1946*

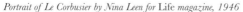

Le Corbusier, of course, *was* Charles-Édouard Jeanneret. When he settled in Paris shortly after World War I, having travelled and sketched extensively, and assisted in the studios of some of the most forward-looking European architects, he set out his creative stall in a magazine, *L'Esprit Nouveau*, founded, with the painter Amédée Ozenfant, under the *nom de plume* Le Corbusier.

In 1923, Le Corbusier published his epochal manifesto *Vers une Architecture* (first translated into English in 1927 as *Towards a New Architecture* – which was not what Le Corbusier nor Ozenfant had meant – by Frederick Etchells, a Vorticist painter who later became a conservation architect specializing in churches, a founding member of the Georgian Group and a stalwart member of the Society for the Protection of Ancient Buildings). It is in this book that Le Corbusier talks of the house, in a much misunderstood phrase, as a 'machine for living'.

Le Corbusier published schemes for ideal new houses and future cities, and was soon building elegant white 'purist' villas for wealthy, artistic clients in and around Paris, culminating in the Villa Savoye (1931). Resting serenely on slender columns, or *piloti*, it made his name as a practising Modern architect. He became feted, admired and, perhaps inevitably, copied.

And here lay Le Corbusier's downfall in terms of his reputation among blimps and fogeys, English-speaking critics for the most who have tended to take sides and spouted in architectural debates before using their eyes and looking. Detractors thought – and still do – that his phrase about houses being machines for living, his plans for high-rise cities set in parks and his, later, love of *beton brut*, or raw concrete, had spawned the prefabricated 'concrete horror' housing estates of Britain, Western Europe, the United States and the former Soviet Union.

While it is true that Le Corbusier's ideas and designs were borrowed, blended and served up in such baleful guises, his own mind was somewhere very different. In fact, it is not difficult to trace a line from his revelatory visit to the Charterhouse of Galluzo, through his ideas of apartment blocks set in parks, through the Villa Savoye, the Pavillon Suisse student hostel (1931), Unité d'Habitation and on to La Tourette. This line can even be extended to Le Petit Cabanon (1951), the tiny wooden cabin he built as a Mediterranean retreat for himself and his wife, Yvonne Gallis, a former fashion model, at Roquebrune-Cap-Martin.

Often reclusive, Le Corbusier was forever trying to recreate the Florentine charterhouse for the modern world. Yes, his long and fecund career was more complex than this pursuit alone, yet it is clear that Le Corbusier's thought and work was hardly synonymous with the cheap-jack local-authority estates of the 1950s to '70s, and schemes to obliterate age-old city centres through car-centric 'comprehensive redevelopment'. Yes, he published outlandish projects to obliterate half of Paris and rebuild the city centre in a new, rational, high-rise form, but this was provocation, a way of testing ideas.

He said silly things, too. In his book *La ville radieuse* (*The Radiant City*, 1935), for example, he described the classical harmony of central Stockholm as 'frightening chaos and saddening monotony'. Although undamaged during World War II – Sweden was a neutral country – post-war architects, planners and politicians plodding in Le Corbusier's shadow ruined much of their city, and continue to do so.

Unité d'Habitation, Marseilles

Le Corbusier can also be criticized for his politics – an opportunist, because he so wanted to build, he worked for the Vichy regime in Nazi-occupied France – yet, by nature, he was apolitical. He was, perhaps, above all an artist, so there had been no need whatsoever to copy him badly, or at all.

Like most highly creative people, his life and thought were complex and contradictory. He loved the idea of a monastic life, but enjoyed society, too. He was a recluse who sought fame. He liked the idea of order and yet harboured a dissenting streak. His forbears, he believed, had been Albigensian (Cathar) purists who, persecuted by Rome for their unorthodox Christian beliefs, had escaped into the Swiss mountains in the thirteenth century.

When Cathars died they swam, metaphysically, into the sun towards the divinity. Le Corbusier had often remarked to friends, 'Wouldn't it be nice to die swimming into the sun?', which is what he did, against doctor's orders, off the coast of Roquebrune-Cap-Martin on 27 August 1965. Salvador Dalí said Le Corbusier's '... recent death filled me with great joy. Mankind will soon be landing on the moon, and just imagine: that buffoon claimed we'd be taking along sacks of reinforced concrete ... Le Corbusier went down for the third time because of his reinforced concrete and his architecture, the ugliest and most unacceptable buildings in the world.'

But, the mercurial artist also sent roses. Le Corbusier, he said, would expect him to behave like a gentleman, and anyway, Dalí felt too cowardly not to. Le Corbusier did indeed stride the world of twentieth-century art and architecture like a concrete Colossus, even though his heart was not far from Renaissance Florence.

City of London Skyline
Nightmare, or happy reflection of the world of high finance?

Until quite recently, the serene dome of St Paul's Cathedral dominated the City of London's skyline. Gathered below and around Wren's beautifully judged design were the towers and spires of the many parish churches this deeply civil architect rebuilt after the 1666 Great Fire of London. Between this lovely play of quietly inventive architectural forms and materials so well suited to the city – Portland stone, lead, soft red Roman brickwork – banks, market halls and pubs, guild halls and chop houses were set clustered on winding streets, narrow alleys and medieval courts.

Despite the Luftwaffe's best attempts to reduce it to rubble during the Blitz of 1940–41, the City survived remarkably intact. There was much rebuilding work, and yet for the next two decades the City retained its special character. Visually, everything seemed to work together: Portland stone buildings, red double-decker buses, red pillar boxes and red fire engines. Food markets continued to flourish near

Painting by Charles Cockerell of St Paul's surrounded by Wren's parish churches

the Stock Exchange. Venerable restaurants, bespoke tailors and family shops thrived alongside imperious-looking banks designed by grand Edwardian architects, while the bells of churches – High, Low and anywhere in between – could still be heard along with those ringing in the cabs of RT and Routemaster buses.

This is the City of London I remember as a boy. It is where my maternal grandfather had his printing works, and where I learned my first lessons in architectural design and history, visiting each and every City church, chapel and the solitary synagogue before my 13th birthday. Today, the City skyline is a disgrace, a wretched, spikey, loud and ill-mannered thing, shouting 'money', its blingy new buildings barging their way into the smallest court or narrowest alley while overshadowing St Paul's. Some of the individual buildings by well-known contemporary architects would be an asset to business parks or to overtly modern city districts like La Défense in Paris.

Not only is St Paul's demeaned, but its chancel now faces a horribly ugly new retail centre bringing all the inevitable shops and beetle-browed 'brands' that can be found in London's West End, and in any British city centre and edge-of-town shopping mall, to one of the few places these could be avoided. It all seems so very provincial. Here, money, bullying and ignorance have done what the Luftwaffe failed to do: destroy the City of London.

St Paul's today, dwarfed by City of London skyscrapers

Villa Capra
Italian home or Renaissance idea?

We all have an idea of home, and what a house should or might be.
And, yet, one of the most famous of all houses is more of an artistic
or intellectual abstraction than what most people would understand
as an everyday house or home. This might seem an odd thing to say,
given that the Villa Capra, or La Rotonda, a masterpiece by Andrea
Palladio – one of the world's greatest architects – has been copied
(if not always very well) over five centuries, and around the world.
Writing this book, I have walked time and again past a contemporary
'Villa Capra' on the Venice Lido, complete with high fences, security
cameras, outdoor lighting and hard-surfaced gardens.

Named after Odorico and Mario Capra, the brothers who later
purchased and completed the house, Villa Capra was commissioned
from Andrea Palladio in 1565–66 by Paolo Almerico, a high-ranking
Vatican official, on his retirement from Rome. Palladio had designed

Exterior showing two symmetrical porticos

a number of remarkable villas for farms in the Veneto, but Almerico's house was to be something quite different – a compact 'palazzo' set on a hilltop overlooking both Vicenza and the countryside around it, and designed as a place of elegant retreat, conversation and contemplation.

Almerico, then, was an ideal client for a house where practical concerns were few and where architecture, decor, books, views and atmosphere mattered most. So, Palladio shaped a symmetrical building planned in the form of a cross, set within an imaginary circle. Each of its four sides was faced with a projecting Ionic entrance portico, like a Roman temple, offering a variety of perfectly framed views and ever-shifting patterns of daylight as the sun moved around the heavens.

The house is centred on an opulent domed circular hall, more ecclesiastical than domestic. Rooms around this are ideally proportioned according to strict mathematical ratios. Service rooms are tucked down below on the ground floor. Walls and ceilings of the *piano nobile* are adorned with *trompe l'oeil* frescos by Alessandro and Giovanni Battista Maganza, Anselmo Canera and, later, by Ludovico Dorigny. These, and the almost Baroque stuccowork over fireplaces – probably the work of Alessandro Vittoria – are as rich, as voluptuous and as colourful as the exterior of the house is essentially modest and clean cut. Rather immodestly, perhaps, sumptuous frescoes in the East Salon portray an allegory of the life of Almerico and his many qualities, among them, modesty, chastity and restraint.

Palladio had intended to crown the house with a high and rather imposing dome. If anything, the appearance of the Villa Capra was improved by Vincenzo Scamozzi, the architect who completed it after the deaths of Palladio and his client. Scamozzi's final design for a low dome guaranteed the simple grace the house exudes from every angle.

Both architects had been influenced by the Pantheon, the domed Roman temple dedicated to all the gods. Scamozzi had even planned to replicate the circular oculus in the centre of the Pantheon's concrete dome. Open to the skies – and so to the heavens and gods – this allowed sunlight and rain to beat down through the temple and out through a great decorated drain in the floor. The Capra brothers, however, were unenthusiastic about the idea: their villa was a private house, not a civic temple.

Palladio's design has captivated the imagination of architects and clients down the centuries. Self-styled Palladian architects built several 'Rotondas' in England in the eighteenth century, while in 1792 Thomas Jefferson proposed a replica as home to the president of the newly independent United States of America. Although his design was unsuccessful, Jefferson, a future US president, built a Villa Capra of his own at his Virginia plantation, Monticello (see page 92).

From the sublime to the crass, Villa Capras continue to be built in the twenty-first century. None has the artistic purity or intellectual rigour of Palladio's original design. Featured in Palladio's famous illustrated manifesto, *I quattro libri dell'architettura*, of 1570, the Villa Capra is as much a theory, an idea, an exemplar and an ideal as it is a home. Because of its compelling design, perfect proportions and undeniable beauty it is, despite this, perhaps the most influential house yet built.

Highly decorated rooms leading from under the central cupola

De Architectura
A philosophy of architecture or DIY manual?

Pushed to recall anything Vitruvius Pollio said in his hugely influential ten books on architecture – *De architectura* – dating from around 15 BCE, most contemporary English-speaking architects will recall the words 'commodity, firmness and delight', the three essential properties of architecture proposed by the Roman architect, as opposed to those applying solely to structure, shelter and building.

These English words are, in fact, an early seventeenth-century rendering of Vitruvius's *firmitas, utilitas* and *venustas* (strength, usefulness and beauty), first appearing in *The Elements of Architecture*, a freestyle and foreshortened translation of *De architectura* by the diplomat Sir Henry Wotton, published in 1624. A full English-language translation of all ten books was not available until 1791.

This in itself is revelatory, for although Vitruvius had been quoted by English architects for well over a century, *De architectura* had always been more of a talisman than a read work. The sole surviving book on architecture handed down to us from ancient Rome, through manuscripts copied by early medieval monks, it is an invaluable document. And yet, far from being a pure treatise on architectural theory, or a polemic, much of it is a wonderfully matter-of-fact presentation of Roman architecture, building and engineering, and, it should be said, all the more fascinating for being so. For, with Vitruvius as our guide, we can imagine what it was like to build in Rome during the last days of the Republic and those of Augustus, the first emperor. From proportion and geometry to descriptions of water pumps, catapults and steam turbines, *De architectura* might be thought of as an architectural encyclopaedia crossed with a Hayne's Manual.

Of Vitruvius himself we know very little, although what contemporary references there are to him by other Roman authors suggest he was an artillery officer in the service of Julius Caesar, and an architect (or chief technician) capable of turning his hand and intelligence to any number of very different projects. In his chapters on the education of architects, Vitruvius expects far more of students than twenty-first-century courses demand. Small wonder the Romans were so good at building.

Although *De architectura* had been known to ecclesiastics, and to rulers like Charlemagne, from the 'Dark Ages' onwards, Vitruvius was only really discovered by architects in the early Renaissance. Poggio Bracciolini, humanist and scholar, came across *De architectura* in the abbey of Saint Gall, Switzerland, in 1414, and it was much discussed on his return to Florence. The manuscript appeared in print in Verona in 1486, followed by a first illustrated edition in Venice in 1511. Translated in the sixteenth century from Latin into Italian, German, Spanish and French, its impact reached across Europe simultaneously with the revival of Roman or classical architecture.

Woodblock print showing labourers creating foundations of a building, illustration from an early printed edition of De architectura

For ingenious, yet practical, men like Leon Battista Alberti, Filippo Brunelleschi and Andrea Palladio, *De architectura* was a professional bible, demonstrating that architecture was a rigorous and scientific calling in the service of both civil society and beauty. Increasingly, it was a book architects and patrons felt they *had* to own, even if they left pages uncut and thus unread.

When anyone asks, how did the Romans achieve so much so quickly, point them in the direction of *De architectura*. However, along with chapters on the slaking of lime for stucco, the decadence of fresco painting, and how to find water, Vitruvius is always minded to tell us that, ultimately, architecture is a discipline in the service of humanity and that its very proportions should be guided by those of the human body, its structures infused with the human soul. Vitruvius was a mechanic, yes, but a philosopher, too.

Man as Measure of All Things, Vitruvian Man by Leonardo da Vinci

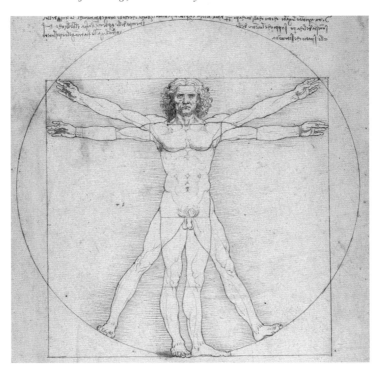

Thomas Jefferson

Ancient Roman or modern
American political values?

As US Minister to France in the 1780s, Thomas Jefferson was able
to catch up first hand with the latest moves in European classical
architecture. In 1768 he had begun work on Monticello, his
plantation home in Virginia. Here, he instigated Palladian design
in America. As his architectural knowledge matured, the future
US president – an ardent republican, democrat and believer in
individual rights – saw Roman classical design as an ideal style for
the new United States.

For Jefferson, Roman architecture – or at least Roman
architecture before Augustus – embodied republican virtues. His
was a Virgilian take on Roman ideals, imagining a land of virtuous,
industrious and independent agrarian people who built civic
monuments and cities infused with these noble values. Retired from
the presidency, he established the University of Virginia. He was
76 at the time and, as yet, as tireless as ever. Jefferson planned and
designed the campus and its buildings. This was centred on a library
influenced by the design of the Pantheon rather than a chapel –
there was none – as Jefferson was a firm believer in the separation
of church and state.

Behind these beautiful Palladian buildings, students tended
vegetable plots, reminding them of their agrarian duties. Again,
Jefferson was thinking of Virgil and his didactic poem the *Georgics*,
published in 29 BCE. Virgil presented a largely idyllic view of the
Italian farmer's life, rooted in a frugal austerity, in hard work in
tune with nature: Rome's greatness was, he suggested, based on this
agrarian idyll.

Intriguingly, the *Georgics* were written with the rise of Octavian
in mind. When the great wars were over, or so the thinking went,
Octavian would settle his battle-hardened veterans on Virgilian
farms, and Italian agriculture would prosper. And yet, it was
Octavian, of course, who killed the Republic, becoming the first
Roman emperor and, unwittingly, heralding an era of economic

growth along with increasingly centralized power, and the absolutist cruelty – and even madness – of his lesser successors. After Augustus, Republican virtues and Virgilian idylls belonged to the past. Now, the architecture of Rome symbolized imperial power and the crushing might of Roman arms. No wonder, then, that authoritarian regimes and absolutist dictators looked to ancient Rome, as Adolf Hitler was to, for architectural inspiration.

In the 1930s, it did seem odd that both Nazi Germany and the democratic United States were building civic monuments in the same heroic style. But, these two opposing nations saw what they wanted to see in the history and architecture of ancient Rome. Where the Germans were thinking of the power, glory and absolutist rule of the Roman Empire, the Americans were looking back through the enlightened eyes of Thomas Jefferson, and thus Palladio, to Virgil and a dream of an ancient and noble republic. Both Hitler and Jefferson were classicists, admirers of Rome and its architecture, but the Bavarian saw an absolutist empire, the American a democratic, republican future in the forms of the past.

The Rotunda, housing the University of Virginia library

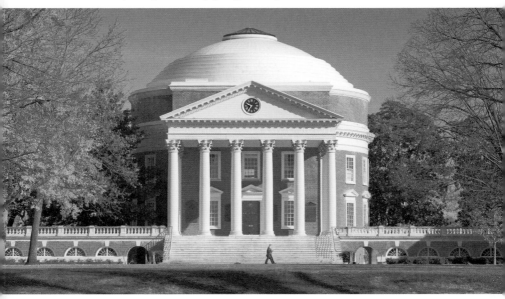

Altes Museum, Berlin

*Symbol of the Prussian Enlightenment,
or foundation stone for Miesian
Modernism?*

Prussian classicism was a refined affair in the age of the eighteenth-century Enlightenment. Inspired at first by ancient Rome, Greek classicism became the favoured architectural style after the defeat of Napoleon Bonaparte in 1815. In part, this was because Napoleon had treated Prussia harshly after his successful invasion of the kingdom, and his march through Berlin in 1806 and Roman classicism was associated with French ambition.

So, when Karl Friedrich Schinkel (1781–1841) was commissioned to design a new public museum in Berlin to display the art collection of the Prussian royal family, he chose a neo-Greek style, creating a serene and chaste Ionic building, completed in 1830, almost devoid of pomp and ornament.

This 'stripped' classicism held a great appeal for the Nazis. To them, Schinkel's Altes Museum had a militaristic, parade-ground feel about it, and so this humane building inspired the work of Hitler's principal architect Albert Speer. Speer saw himself as an architect continuing in the spirit of Schinkel, yet this highly intelligent man bought 100 per cent into the dark world of Nazism. In doing so, he even brought humanists like Schinkel into disrepute after World War II.

I can remember hearing Schinkel's work being described as 'proto-Nazi' on several occasions while working for the *Architectural Review* in the 1980s. It was, of course, nothing of the sort; Schinkel's own style graduated to neo-Gothic and then what might be seen as a kind of functionalism or perhaps, at a pinch, a proto-Modernism that was to prove heavily influential for Mies van der Rohe (see page 15). If anything, it was more Bauhaus than Bunker.

Domed interior with colonnade

Les Espaces d'Abraxas, Marne-la-Vallée

Versailles for the people, or Postmodern Parisian ghetto?

When in the late 1970s Ricardo Bofill's Taller de Arquitectura, a quixotic Barcelona-based practice, was commissioned to design new mass housing in Marne-la-Vallée, a new town on the fringe of Paris, Sarcelles was the enemy, the French housing project to target and fight against.

Designed by Jacques Henri-Labourdette and Roger Boileau and built between 1955 and 1976, Sarcelles was a colossal concrete

Central piazza with 'Triumphal Arch' set against an even grander block behind

Parisian housing project – a kind of mass-produced, technocratic and artless interpretation of the work of Le Corbusier – providing 12,638 new homes in what, from the air or the window of a passing train, can look like a single, soulless megastructure formed of horizontal and concrete rectangles.

As a reaction to Sarcelles, which had been much criticized in France for its 'inhumane' design, Bofill proposed a Versailles for the People at Marne-la-Vallée, employing new techniques in pre-cast concrete technology to manufacture huge Postmodern classical panels that, clipped to the frames of his giant apartment blocks, would give these the appearance of noble palaces for the New Town proletariat.

More than this, the apartment blocks forming Les Espaces d'Abraxas would be laid out on the notional plan of an imperial Roman city. So here is a triumphal arch, housing 20 flats, a great circus of more flats, and a colossal imperial palace, of sorts, containing hundreds more flats. When complete in 1983, Les Espaces d'Abraxas was a *coup de théâtre*, an audacious housing project that confounded Bofill's fellow architects, critics and residents alike. But, if the aim had been high spirited and noble, the scheme was flawed. Behind those dramatic pilasters, cornices and artfully broken concrete pediments were hundreds of rather drab apartments, many with views into dark and vertiginous courtyards and service alleys.

In its own way Les Espaces d'Abraxas proved to be as sorry as Sarcelles. Weathered concrete panels are not so very grand 30 years on, while poor maintenance, a lack of shops and basic services and, yes, the scheme's inhuman scale have all pricked Bofill's heroic dream. It was no wonder that Terry Gilliam chose Les Espaces d'Abraxas as a backdrop for his dystopian film *Brazil* (1985).

Taller de Arquitectura produced several more gigantic and provocative Postmodern classical concrete housing schemes. On paper they seemed so very exciting and they have been, undeniably, the stuff of photographers' dreams. But, were they really better than Sarcelles as homes for people, many of them immigrants new to France, with no choice in where they lived?

Dymaxion House
A Model T Ford house or an eccentric one-off design?

Richard Buckminster Fuller had a dream: of a house made of lightweight industrial materials that could be mass-produced on a factory assembly line like the Model T Ford. And, even better, the low-cost 'Dymaxion' house would be flown to anywhere freedom-loving American citizens chose to live in their great country.

Born in 1895 in Milton, Massachusetts, Fuller was a dreamer. Expelled twice from Harvard, he took on such unlikely jobs as a labourer in a stockyard and commander of a crash rescue boat in World War I before finding funds (he had great charm) to develop various prototypes for factory-made homes and three land-bound versions of a proposed flying car. Fuller believed both Dymaxion house and car would sell like hotcakes, apple pie and Model T Fords.

Looking perhaps a little too much like circular grain bins or, in retrospect, a flying saucer from Ed Wood's *Plan 9 from Outer Space*, the Dymaxion prototypes garnered publicity without generating

Shining Dymaxion house prototype

investment or sales. Although ingeniously planned, with built-in kitchens, storage and bathrooms, the use of rainwater for anything other than drinking and cooking, and naturally air-conditioned through convection-driven roof ventilators, Fuller's prototypes were considered too eccentric to live in comfortably: rooms with curved walls have always been notoriously difficult to furnish and decorate.

There was a brief moment immediately after World War II when a revamped version of the Dymaxion house – the Wichita house – might have taken off. The Beech Aircraft Company of Wichita, Kansas, promoted the idea widely and was said to have received 37,000 enquiries from potential buyers. The experience of four years of industrial warfare had introduced millions of Americans to the virtues of new materials and technology. Each house, offering 93 square metres (1,000 square feet) of living accommodation yet weighing just 3 tonnes, and comprising 3,000 aircraft industry components, would be delivered on site in a steel tube. It would take ten men just two days to erect it. The total cost? Just $6,500, or the price of a new Cadillac.

In April 1946, the Wichita project was trumpeted by *Fortune* magazine. What could possibly go wrong? Everything, really. When Beech Aircraft suggested changes to the design and materials for mass production, Fuller walked away, categorically refusing to compromise his design. And, that was the end of the Dymaxion house.

The only Dymaxion house ever lived in was a hybrid, constructed from the two pre-war Fuller prototypes by William Graham, a businessman, who worked them into an extension of his lake-front ranch house in Andover, Kansas. In 1990, Graham's family donated the house and a bundle of unused Dymaxion components to the Henry Ford Museum at Dearborn, Michigan. Restored, as far as possible, to its original state, the Dymaxion house now resides indoors in a spot-lit gallery, a lonely curiosity rather than a model for twentieth-century mass housing. Meanwhile, Henry Ford, Fuller's hero, had built 15 million Model Ts.

This was not quite the end of the story. Fuller had been unable to realize his dream of mass-produced Dymaxion houses reached by airborne Dymaxion cars, but he channelled his fascination with lightweight, prefabricated structures into the design of his geodesic dome. By the time of his death in 1983, more than 300,000 of these Space Age structures had been assembled for any number of purposes around the world, some of them delivered by helicopter.

National Assembly Building, Dhaka

Self-conscious antiquity or timeless design?

When Louis Kahn, a young American architect, toured Europe in 1928, five years after the publication of Le Corbusier's epoch-making Modernist manifesto *Vers une architecture*, what he chose to see were not the latest French and German white concrete villas but the massive stone walls of medieval French towns and venerable Scottish castles.

Kahn (1901–74) – born Itze-Leib Schmuilowsky in Estonia – stored the memory of these solid buildings in his mind's eye for a quarter of a century before creating a new form of Modern architecture from the mid-1950s, which included the National Assembly Building, Dhaka, one of the greatest buildings of all time.

Rising from the shores of an artificial lake, the home of the Bangladeshi parliament has the feel of some heroic building of the age of ancient Rome, and yet it is quite different from anything built before it – except, that is, for Kahn's own work. This utterly magnificent building is formed of a number of massive building blocks gathered around a great central octagon. Composed of Plato's universal elements – tetrahedron, icosahedron, dodecahedron, octahedron and cube, representing fire, water, ether, air and earth – there are committee rooms, offices, a library, restaurant and mosque gathered around a lofty, octagonal parliamentary chamber, soaring to a high parabolic concrete vault in the guise of what looks like a star beaming with light from the floor below.

Each of these blocks is made of rough-shuttered concrete, inset with bands of white marble. Each is divided from one another and the assembly chamber by courtyards open to the air and yet joined together by cool, high-vaulted concrete passageways and stairs that ascend and descend around the complex like an Escher drawing.

From the lake, gardens and streets beyond, the building – designed between 1962 and 1973, and completed in 1982 – is all of a piece, belying its complex and internal spaces. Plays of sunlight,

Complex and cavernous interior

mist and water change the colour and feel of the exterior of this mesmerizing building, while inside, daylight revels in 1,001 games and shadow-play dances. This mighty building is both solid and ethereal, built to delight and endure.

From the very beginning its political fortune was fickle. Commissioned from Kahn in 1962 as a home for the Pakistani parliament, in 1971 what had been East Pakistan since 1947 had become the independent republic of Bangladesh. And yet, rooted in both the timeless architecture of the ancient world, and the symbolism and building traditions of India over many centuries, Kahn's building would have, and will, outlast any number of fleeting political regimes. It seems unlikely that an earthquake would destroy it, much less a flood.

What Kahn demonstrated in Dhaka is that a building can be of its time and place and yet all but timeless. He showed something else, too. Bangladesh was, and is, a poor country. To build a monumental parliamentary complex at a cost of $32 million – double the proposed budget – when millions of Bangladeshis had little to eat and barely any shelter, might have seemed plain wrong. And yet, millions of Bangladeshis are proud of this building today. Great architecture can instil a sense of hope, pride and resilience in people, especially when it truly belongs yet transcends purely everyday concerns.

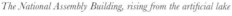

The National Assembly Building, rising from the artificial lake

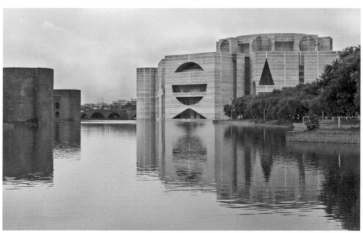

Sinan the Magnificent
Brilliant bureaucrat or great architect?

Mimar Sinan (1489–1588) was appointed court architect to the Ottoman emperor Suleiman the Great when he was 50 years old. He then held this office for very nearly half a century, during which time he built an accredited 394 buildings and structures, from mosques and madrasas, aqueducts and bridges, public baths and fountains, to hospitals and mausoleums.

Known as Joseph in an earlier life, Sinan is thought to have been the son of a Greek Christian stonemason. Conscripted into the Ottoman imperial Jannisary corps (an elite force composed mostly of former Christians), Sinan converted to Islam and rose quickly to high office, fighting in many of the major battles that saw Suleiman rise to power.

A fighter and a military engineer, Sinan had the skills, energy and determination to succeed – skills that were also to make him a dynamic and supremely efficient architect. He was not a theorist. As court architect, he ran an office in Istanbul some 500 strong, dispatching standardized designs for mosques and military buildings

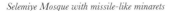

Selemiye Mosque with missile-like minarets

across the empire. He was an engineer and technician, a bureaucrat and diplomat. In today's terms he might be seen as the CEO of a major international company.

And yet, Sinan was also a great artist; through diplomatic channels he certainly knew of the work of Michelangelo in Rome, another tireless and efficient technocrat. Sinan's Selemiye Mosque in Edirne and Suleymaniye Mosque in Istanbul are superb designs, vast and numinous buildings bringing complex forms and geometries into singular harmony under guiding domes that appear to float above rather than bear down on the structures below.

What we know of Sinan on a personal level comes mostly from Ottoman hagiographies. Stand, though, in the centre of the Selimiye or Suleymaniye Mosques and his magnificence is unquestionable. What an impeccable technocrat. What a brilliant architect.

Looking up into the dome of Selimiye Mosque

John Portman
Futurist architect or real estate developer?

Changing planes in Atlanta some years ago on my way back from Texas to London, I booked overnight into the Atlanta Marriot Marquis. I knew that this 52-storey hotel, opened in 1985, was meant to be one of the world's most spectacular, yet nothing quite prepared me for the experience of its lobby at night, soaring up, along with banks of glass elevators, into what seemed to be outer space. No wonder American film directors have flocked here over the years to film science-fiction thrillers.

Curiously, the exterior of the Atlanta Marriot Marquis resembles almost any other downtown concrete skyscraper. Yes, its structure billows out towards its base as if the tower was somehow pregnant, but you would never guess it featured such a remarkable interior. This, though, is the trademark of the spectacular and controversial designs of the Atlanta architect John C. Portman Jr (born in 1924 in Walhalla, South Carolina), who – perhaps more than any other modern architect – has combined his professional role with that of downtown property developer.

The soaring lobby of the Atlanta Marriott Marquis

Portman's first atrium hotel, the 22-storey Hyatt Regency Atlanta, opened in 1967. It certainly caught critics' eyes, although it was hard for most to decide whether this was a great step into the future or a commercial building displaying just a bit too much swagger and braggadocio. It was certainly exciting, especially with Polaris, a revolving restaurant named after the famous submarine-launched Lockheed ballistic nuclear missile, perched like a hovering flying saucer on top of the concrete skyscraper.

Showing how quickly Portman's Atlanta developed in the following decades, Polaris was closed in 2004, partly because what had been sensational 360-degree views over the city and surrounding countryside were now of the many concrete and glass towers that had rocketed up around it since 1967. Happily, the restaurant reopened in 2014. Today's diners enjoy views of the brightly lit, skyscraper-packed city centre, while, intriguingly, the restaurant aims to be as 'green' as possible: it has its own colony of bees producing honey for the kitchen, and a roof garden growing vegetables high above the city's sidewalks.

Although criticized for turning the streets of city centres into clusters of concrete towers, John Portman has undoubtedly brought excitement and delight to those using his buildings. The question raised by his prodigious portfolio of city towers is this: can we have skyscrapers and city centres pedestrians can enjoy, too? Fifty years ago, the answer might have been 'no', or 'not exactly', even if Manhattan had proved such a thing was possible. However, Portman's latest towers do address streets and sidewalks rather than skylines and profit curves only.

Today Portman's career remains controversial. As chairman of Portman Holdings, a powerful real-estate company, should he be an architect, too? In the 1960s, property developers tended to seek out big-name architects, working hard to persuade them to design profitable downtown skyscrapers. Half a century on, big-name architects woo big-shot developers, who have become the real power brokers – commercially and artistically, and for better or worse – in the design of city centres worldwide. Portman might be seen as being well ahead of the game, a professional with great panache who brought these two camps together. In any case, I defy anyone not to enjoy a drink in the Polaris restaurant and cocktail bar, or not to be thrilled when looking up and up into the lobby of that vertiginous cathedral of capitalism, the Atlanta Marriot Marquis.

Temples of Khajuraho, India
Religious experience or erotic playground?

Kama Sutra in sandstone. This has been the opinion of many visitors who make the long journey to the tenth- to eleventh-century temple complex at Khajuraho in central India. The surviving 25 Hindu and Jain temples, set between eucalyptus trees and bright bougainvillea today, are famed for their erotic sculptures, depicting athletic sex acts that would have most tourists, should they try to put these into practice, in the casualty wards of hospitals.

Although there are dozens of books of photographs celebrating these remarkable images, the erotic sculptures of Khajuraho comprise a small percentage of the thousands that encrust and animate these extraordinary temples. What we know of them is limited. They were erected, it seems, over a century or so, during the Rajput Chandela dynasty, whose kingdom was the Bundelkhand region, in today's Madhya Pradesh. The Chandela kings owned diamond mines that presumably paid for this forest of exquisite religious towers.

It seems likely that the temples, decorated with sculptures representing daily life, farming and warfare, were a celebration of life

The Kandariya Mahadeva Temple, with the Jagadambi Temple beyond

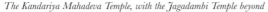

and reincarnation in all their richness. It has also been suggested that they are a monument to the marriage of the god Shiva – destroyer and creator – and Parvati, goddess of love, fertility and devotion.

The sculpture of these temples, however, should be seen as all of a piece, even though groups of young men can be found, hot off Indian tourist coaches, sniggering lewdly at reliefs depicting love-making as if these were illustrations from crude 'men's' magazines on the top shelves of Mumbai bookstalls. The temples declined from the time of thirteenth-century Muslim invasions. Over the following 500 years, many were defaced and others destroyed. Fortunately, even today, Khajuraho is remote, and as vegetation smothered the temples, they all but disappeared from view, although they were known to local people.

The complex was 'rediscovered' in 1838 by the young Captain T. S. Burt of the Royal Bengal Engineers on a surveying expedition through central India. It is easy to imagine Burt's surprise when vegetation was cut back and the '*Kama Sutra* in sandstone' was unveiled in all its fertile glory. From 1904, the temples were systematically restored under the sympathetic direction of the Archaeological Survey of India. Here, architecture, nature, eroticism and spirituality are intertwined: they were intended to be one and the same thing.

Detail of erotic 'Kama Sutra' temple sculpture

Liverpool Metropolitan Cathedral
Sixties period piece or canonic place of worship?

The new Roman Catholic Metropolitan Cathedral of Christ the King rocketed up over the Mersey skyline in just five years. To some, this adventurous design had the look of a NASA Gemini space capsule. To others, it resembled a giant concrete-and-stone tent. Because of Liverpool's large Irish Catholic population, it was nicknamed 'Paddy's Wigwam'.

Whatever the image its architect, Frederick Gibberd (1908–84), had in mind – his recent work had included the new Jet Age terminals at Heathrow Airport – this was a truly striking building, a visual thrill when it opened in May 1967. It commanded Liverpool's Brownlow Hill, facing Sir Giles Gilbert Scott's vast and still incomplete red sandstone-faced neo-Gothic cathedral, which had been under construction since 1904. It revolutionized the image of the Catholic Church in England. It was a powerful marriage of adventurous modern architecture, structural engineering, art, design and craft.

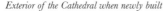

Exterior of the Cathedral when newly built

Sixteen concrete buttresses (or tent poles) support a lantern filled with glorious red, blue and yellow stained glass – representing the Holy Trinity – designed by John Piper and made by Patrick Reyntiens. This bathes the circular nave and the altar at its centre in washes of numinous colour. It is an enchanting, even mystical, experience to walk around the perimeter to the central nave and to see one's hands and other people's faces change colour, while looking up into the lantern is a glimpse of architectural sorcery and perhaps even heaven itself.

Thirteen chapels were placed around and between the buttresses, each adorned by the work of a litany of distinguished modern artists and craft workers. Was it all too good to be true? Yes. The competition for the cathedral's design announced in 1959 called for a design that could be realized within five years, at a cost of no more than one million pounds.

This was asking for little more than a miracle, although such ambitious parsimony was understandable. Three earlier schemes for a Catholic cathedral had all come to nothing. Only one section – the Lady Chapel – of a lofty neo-Gothic cathedral designed in 1853 by Edward Welby Pugin was built, in Everton. This was used as a parish church and demolished in the 1980s. Edwin Lutyens's costly proposal for a domed cathedral, begun in 1933, got no further than its crypt (completed after World War II), while a scaled-down version of the same building by Adrian Gilbert Scott dating from the early 1950s was an awkward-looking affair. In any case, it would have cost four times as much as the Church wanted to spend.

The great rush to build in a brand new style, however, led to expensive structural flaws, and the cathedral cannot be said to have been truly finished until 2003. This, though, was a hugely optimistic building, opened in a year when so much – whether in design, engineering or popular culture – seemed so fresh, fast and brimming with energy and colour.

In 1967, Liverpool could be reached from London in record time by the latest 100mph blue-and-white Inter City electric trains. The Beatles released *Sgt. Pepper's Lonely Hearts Club Band*. There were crazes for inflatable plastic furniture and disposable paper clothes. Fashion boutiques flowered, Britain's first 'High-Tech' building – the Reliance Controls Factory by Team Four (Richard Rogers, Su Brumwell, Norman Foster and Wendy Cheeseman) – opened in

Swindon, and Concorde made its public debut. In the same year, though, *Apollo 1* caught fire on its Cape Kennedy launchpad, killing its crew, and the Vietnam War raged pointlessly. There were riots in Newark and Detroit. The *Torrey Canyon* oil tanker sank off the coast of Cornwall, causing an environmental catastrophe, and Thamesmead, a brutal concrete new town screaming 'alienation' and 'dystopia', was under construction in southeast London. The first houses were occupied the following year. They leaked.

Liverpool's Catholic cathedral was a child of its times. The project was hurried, the budget unrealistic. Its teething problems did little to instil confidence in Modern architecture in Britain. It has, though, matured over the decades, evolving into a fine and unforgettable building, with one of the most original and moving interiors shaped in the 1960s.

Ethereal stained-glass lantern crowning the central altar

TWA Flight Center, New York
Future or past of commercial flight?

The New York architect and historian Robert Stern has dubbed it 'the Grand Central of the Jet Age'. Eero Saarinen's soaring, swooping concrete terminal at New York's JFK Airport remains a wonder of its era, a jewel of a building and one that has been impossible not to fall in love with since it opened in 1962. Yet this thrilling building closed in December 2001, when Trans World Airlines filed for bankruptcy. Ever since, and dwarfed by surrounding new developments, it has been looking for a new role. It might yet reopen as a hotel, its vaulted central space shaping what would certainly be one of the world's most striking and desirable lobbies.

A triumph of Jet Age design, the TWA Flight Center represents a tragic turn in the way we have relearned to fly since 1962. A need for increased security, an ever-growing number of passengers and the transformation of airports into shopping malls means that small, yet perfectly formed, terminals like Saarinen's are out of place and out of time. The terminal still speaks of a future, but not the future the airline industry has chosen to take.

The highly expressive interior when new

John Pawson
Slight minimalist or quiet visionary?

In the early 1980s, the writer Bruce Chatwin, a fellow Yorkshireman, introduced John Pawson to Le Thoronet, the late twelfth-century Cistercian abbey in Provence. Ever since, this spare and exquisitely beautiful abbey has remained the touchstone, the guiding principle, of the architect's work.

Born in 1949 to Methodist parents – his father ran a successful textile business – John Pawson is not strictly an architect, having dropped out of an educational system he found pointless after several years trekking through Asia and teaching English in Japan, where he also worked for the craftsman-designer Shiro Kuramata.

Chatwin was one of Pawson's first clients, the commission a tiny flat in Eaton Place, Belgravia. Bare, minimal, pure and white, it set the tone for Pawson's work. What this socially adroit architect offered the world of 1980s architecture, and its clients, was a breath of Provençal Cistercian and pure mountain air.

At the time, silly Postmodern design held far too much sway in Britain, as in the United States – all lurid colours, incongruous shapes

Chaste refectory of the abbey Our Lady of Novy Dvur

and unconvincing playfulness. From an aesthetic point of view, Pawson's single-minded purism took eighties design for a cleansing bath in an ice-cold lake. His minimalist aesthetic, underpinned by a love of art, craftsmanship, natural materials and the play of daylight on unadorned surfaces was both refreshing and captivating.

His style, however, was also perceived as a new form of luxury by clients who, often very wealthy and hardly ascetic, liked the idea of splashing out on homes, art galleries and hotels that looked both sparse and worth millions of dollars. This slightly uncomfortable duality has characterized Pawson's work: the rich wanting to live and work in monkish spaces that also shout (or should this be whisper?) modesty and refinement.

And then, quite out of the blue, Pawson's story turned full circle. As strange and as comic as it might seem, real-life Cistercian monks from the Czech Republic just happened to be in Manhattan, where they greatly admired the style and ersatz religious atmosphere of Pawson's new Calvin Klein store on Fifth Avenue. This led to a commission to extend, rebuild and shape a new monastic church for the Abbey of Our Lady of Novy Dvur in Bohemia. It was, of course, the ideal project for Pawson, and he lived up to the challenge, creating spare and harmonious spaces for those who really do believe that 'minimalism' and perfectionism are next to godliness, while maintaining that only God is truly perfect.

From the design of tableware to apartments and houses for the ostentatiously unostentatious rich, and then a Cistercian abbey, Pawson has managed to square a circle in his career between architectural desire and integrity. Ultimately, his work – which is very much his own – is often as beautiful and as taut as a Japanese haiku, or daylight touching plain walls, floors and vaults through simple windows pierced through cool stonework; and this is surely enough to ensure any serious architect's reputation.

Postmodernism
Modernism redeemed or duped?

In some ways, it was Mies van der Rohe's Seagram Building (1958; see page 17) on Manhattan's Park Avenue that set the Postmodern beach ball rolling. Aloof, exquisite, self-referential and all but impossible to copy except badly, it could be read from the start as both the apogee of Modernism and its tipping point.

In 1962 the American architect Robert Venturi wrote an essay while in Rome, published four years later as *Complexity and Contradiction in Architecture*. Where Mies wrote 'Less is more', Venturi contradicted the German-American master, saying, equally pithily, 'Less is a bore'. Functionalism, opined Venturi, had gone too far. Architects needed to look again at history, to shape buildings that drew in lifestyles and manners from an abundance of sources around them. Heck, they should even look again at the work of Edwin Lutyens.

Complexity and Contradiction was a provocative, thoughtful and hugely enjoyable book, and for many of its architect readers, a necessary one, too. Mies was not bad, of course, but the sheer

'Mother's House', Chestnut Hill, Philadelphia

number of lacklustre copies of Mies buildings in cities around the world by the mid-1960s was depressing. Equally, functionalism had mass-produced apparently inescapable and determinedly grim concrete housing estates in a global profusion of cracks, leaks, damp and sheer human misery. Far from liberating humankind, Modern architecture could be seen as destroying cities and causing a state of ennui underpinned with unhappiness.

With his wife and practice partner, Denise Scott Brown, Venturi followed up in 1972 with *Learning from Las Vegas*, another clever, challenging book that said, 'Main Street is almost all right'. In other words, architects and planners would do well to learn from the everyday streets and buildings under their exclusive noses. Meanwhile, in 1964, Venturi had designed and built a house for his mother in Chestnut Hill, Philadelphia, that, although modest and modern in many ways, caused a stir in architectural circles. Its facade took the form of a giant split pediment rising straight up from the ground. Was this a play on sixteenth-century Mannerism as practised by Michelangelo in Rome and Giulio Romano in Mantua, or simply a provocation?

Venturi's and Scott Brown's influence on architecture and design should not be underestimated, although they hated being labelled Postmodernists. This is understandable, given the rash of jokey and downright daft buildings, beginning in the United States, that were to spread virulently through the worlds of architecture and design in the 1970s and '80s. Candy-coloured buildings decked out in cartoon-like classical details and apparently designed to affront all notions of conventional good taste popped up in city centres like the big tops of travelling circuses or striped booths of Punch and Judy shows. The difference is that the buildings were intended to be permanent. Jokes, however, tend to lose their punch over the years and, by the late 1980s, Postmodern architecture and design seemed very unfunny indeed.

Venturi himself attempted to give his 'inclusive' or mannerist style some gravitas with the design of the Sainsbury Wing of the National Gallery (1991), facing London's Trafalgar Square. Here, elisions and plays of classical detailing were partnered with office-like glass curtain walls and other Po-mo tricks. Despite Portland stone dressing, the building looked as uncomfortable as a nightclub bouncer in a dinner jacket and dickie-bow tie.

Several great Modern architects had already moved a long way from functionalism and the Bauhaus by the time Venturi wrote *Complexity and Contradiction*. Le Corbusier, Alvar Aalto, Louis Kahn and Eero Saarinen were just the most famous and talented of those who had shaped new forms of Modern architecture that, ultimately, were to have more influence on twenty-first-century design than gimcrack Postmodernism. A fascinating diversion, Po-mo made architects and designers sit up and think, yet proved unable to produce a convincing body of work, as had Italian Mannerism, Baroque or the Arts and Crafts movement before it.

Kengo Kuma's M2 Building, Tokyo, capped with overscaled Ionic column

Fallingwater
Keepsake or liability?

Asked for his occupation in a court of law, Frank Lloyd Wright (1867–1959) replied 'The world's greatest architect'. His wife remonstrated with him. 'I had no choice, Olgivanna', he told her, 'I was under oath.'

The cocksure Wright was a master of the one-line quip. He told a client who phoned to complain of rain leaking from the roof of her new house onto the dining table where she was sitting to 'move the chair'. Thinking of Mies, he said, 'Less is only more where more is no good'. On seeing his tall assistant, William Wesley Peters, inside one of his latest and rather low-ceilinged houses, he barked, 'Sit

Exterior of the house above the waterfall

down, Wes, you're ruining the scale of my architecture'. Of himself, this very original American architect bragged, 'Early in life I had to choose between honest arrogance and hypocritical humility. I chose the former and have seen no reason to change.'

Wright lived a roller-coaster life. He abandoned his first wife, Kitty, and five children and fled to Europe with his mistress and client, Mamah Cheney. On their return to the US, Mamah and her children were murdered at his home, Taliesin, which burned down (and Wright rebuilt) twice. His autobiography, a best seller, was the inspiration for Ayn Rand's novel *The Fountainhead*, made into a dramatic film with Gary Cooper in the lead role.

Wright's architecture could be something of a fairground ride, too. When questioned over the heights of the galleries in his sensational Solomon R. Guggenheim Museum on Fifth Avenue, he said, 'Cut the paintings in half'. 'A doctor', he joked, more than half-seriously, 'can bury his mistakes, but an architect can only advise his clients to plant vines.'

Designed as a weekend retreat for the wealthy Pittsburgh store-owners Edgar and Liliane Kaufmann, Fallingwater (1939) was built on an outcrop of rock over a waterfall at Bear Run, Pennsylvania. Its three floors took the form of ambitious 19-metre (62-foot) concrete cantilevers, thrust 5 metres (16 $^{1}/_{2}$ feet) over the fast-falling water from a rock where the Kaufmanns had long enjoyed picnics. This was a dramatic and costly move, yet Fallingwater was a truly beautiful design and the Kaufmanns could well afford the $155,000 – a huge sum at the time; the budget had been $30,000 – they paid for the house of their dreams.

In 1997, scaffolding was put in place to stop Fallingwater falling down. Four years later, a repair programme was announced. It would cost $11.5 million to right the wrongs of those daring cantilevers. Robert Silman, a structural engineer from New York who had already worked on seven Wright houses, planned the work. 'This doesn't diminish the architectural brilliance of his buildings', he said. 'One after the other, they are absolutely breathtaking.' And this is why, Fallingwater – expensive to build and maintain – will never be short of funds. Wright's architecture could indeed be a liability, yet those who choose to live in Wright homes love them, and, as experience tells us, the price of true love can be very costly indeed.

Thermal Baths, Vals
Building into landscape, or landscape into building?

'Mountain, stone, water – building in the stone, building with the stone, into the mountain, building out of the mountain, being inside the mountain – how can the implications and the sensuality of the association of these words be interpreted architecturally?' Peter Zumthor asked himself this convoluted question when asked to design a thermal spa for a hotel owned by the community of Vals in Graubünden, a mountainous region of southeast Switzerland.

Meeting of granite geometries, architectural and natural, Vals

Completed in 1996, this rigorous, yet mystical and wholly enchanting building is one of the quiet architectural wonders of the world. Set against a backdrop of mountains, the baths have a powerful architectural presence rising in tiers of silver-grey quartzite facings over a concrete frame, punctuated by deep-set windows and openings. Inside, they prove to be an interlocking sequence of chambers, or individual buildings, housed behind the quartzite walls under a roof constructed from concrete beams and glass.

Daylight filters down through a theatrical yet poetic steamy half-darkness, across stone walls and floors and other surfaces, and fittings of brass, chrome, velvet and leather. Water bubbles. People appear and disappear like characters in a David Lynch film. All is a sensory delight. And, when you need daylight and the mountains again, the building opens up at roof level, views framed by powerful architectural elements.

Cavern, quarry, man-made mountain, archaeological site, Roman bath … Vals conjures such images among many others. Here, architecture is landscape, while the landscape has clearly influenced the architecture. This is a building from the 1990s, yet somehow out of time. It has the feeling of some ancient monument, a temple or a shrine to a mystical water goddess, and yet its design is logical and crystal clear. The baths are also massively and meticulously crafted.

Peter Zumthor (born 1943) is the son of a Swiss cabinetmaker. He trained as a furniture maker and conservation architect before setting up his own practice, crafting just one fine building at a time, including the haunting St Benedict Chapel (1988) at Sumvitg, Graubünden, which replaced a Baroque parish church destroyed in an avalanche. More than almost any living architect, Zumthor has the ability to create a sense of timelessness in his work, realized through a love and knowledge of the property of materials, whether timber shingles and ancient stones, or the latest developments in concrete and glass. His work is modern, it does not toy with historical forms, and yet it has its place with architecture down the ages. Zumthor's buildings face nature anew while enhancing and truly belonging to it.

Metabolism
Japanese fashion statement or truly radical design?

On 15 August 1945, following the Battle of Okinawa, the Soviet invasion of the Japanese puppet state of Manchukuo and the dropping of atomic bombs on Hiroshima and Nagasaki, Emperor Hirohito gave a rare public speech. Recorded rather badly on a phonograph, the 'Jewel Voice Broadcast' was delivered in a piping classical Japanese few people could readily understand, over the strains of portentous music. 'The war situation', said the emperor, in one of the greatest understatements of all time, 'has developed not necessarily to Japan's advantage'.

Physically, politically, militarily and philosophically, Japan was wrecked. It was hardly surprising, then, that young architects considering how to rebuild the country looked to old, new and even international Marxist ideas to plan for a very different future. The Metabolist group, which launched its manifesto in 1960 after several

Exterior of the Nakagin Capsule Tower, Tokyo

years of discussion between architects and social and political theorists, had originally intended to call itself the Burnt Ash School. From the embers of a firebombed country, a new architecture would emerge, drawing on the latest ideas in science and technology as well as on nature and the age-old Japanese tradition of renewing old buildings. The concerns of the disgraced imperial era would be bypassed and hopefully forgotten.

In a biological manner, Metabolist buildings would spawn. Like organisms they would grow and shape megastructures and even entire new cities. Because they would be constructed from prefabricated, clip-together components, they could shrink when necessary, the idea being a form of architecture and urbanism highly responsive to change. Many of the idealistic designs, which were to remain on paper or else in the guise of scale models, resemble crystals or molecular structures. Wholly intriguing, they also seem ultimately inhumane, as if young Japanese architects were designing for ants or termites rather than human beings.

Under the guidance of Kenzo Tange, who had won international acclaim for his 1949 design for the Hiroshima Peace Memorial Museum (1955), young architects including Kiyonori Kikutake, Kisho Kurokawa and Fumihiko Maki proposed imaginative schemes,

Cramped interior of a capsule apartment

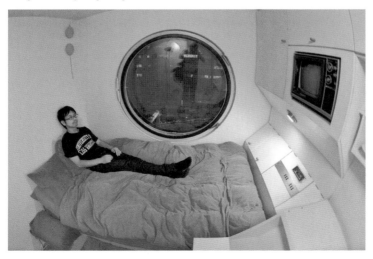

including an Ocean City that would float on the seas, free from the threat of war, and various forms of 'megastructure' cities that would solve the problem of post-war housing.

In the event, only a very few Metabolist designs were built. The best known is most probably Kurokawa's Nakagin Capsule Tower in Ginza, Tokyo. Completed in a rush in 1972, this striking structure comprises 140 lightweight prefabricated steel living capsules plugged into a pair of interconnected 11- and 13-storey concrete service towers. Each capsule is tiny, offering Tokyo's bachelor 'salarymen' a studio fitted out with the very latest services and gadgets, including air conditioning, reel-to-reel tape recorders, hi-fi and a bathroom the size of an aircraft lavatory. The view out across an elevated road was through a single porthole.

The idea seems logical, and the building remains an act of faith, a design looking to a 'Metabolist' future that was never to be. Residents took against the constraints of the tower. By 2015, few lived there and the building was in a poor state of repair.

At the time of the construction of the Nakagin Capsule Tower, however, Japan's economic and technological recovery was remarkable. The 1964 Olympics were a showcase of radical new design, from Kenzo Tange's stadium – a marriage of the very latest lightweight engineering technology and traditional Japanese forms – to the sensational new high-speed Shinkansen 'bullet trains' that were to revolutionize rail travel worldwide. Cameras, cars, consumer electronics, films, graphics and fashion were all on a roll. Somehow, though, the idea of plug-in capsule towers, vertical or horizontal megastructures, and floating cities, although all very fascinating, proved to be not necessarily to Japan's advantage.

Eladio Dieste

*Doing too much with too little, or
great architecture on a shoestring?*

I met Eladio Dieste just once, and through an unexpected route. I
had been to Buenos Aires to see Livio Dante Porta, the innovative
Argentinian steam locomotive engineer who, late in the era of TGVs
and Eurostars, was developing highly efficient steam engines burning
the cheapest and least polluting fuels. In a discussion concerning
other Latin American engineers working along apparently different
and yet parallel or even converging lines, Eladio Dieste's name was
mentioned. I was shown photographs of the brick shell vaults of a
church some 40 kilometres (25 miles) from Montevideo, and these
pointed me in the direction of Uruguay and to an extraordinary
man whose talent, like Porta's, has yet to be fully recognized.

Born in 1917, Dieste trained as an engineer. He became an
architect not through qualifications but through building. His first
independent commission was the church I had glimpsed in those
photographs handed around in a house in Buenos Aires. This is the

Rolling brick roof vaults of Christ the Worker church, Estación Atlántida, Uruguay

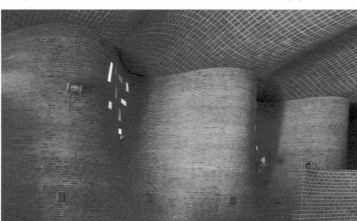

Church of Christ the Worker and Our Lady of Lourdes, completed in 1960 in Estación Atlántida, a formless suburb of a small resort town on the Atlantic coast of southern Uruguay. Curious from the outside, inside Christ the Worker is a gem. Here, undulating brick walls support rippling reinforced brick vaults, rolling like an Atlantic coaster from one end of the nave to the other. Vaults and walls are day-lit from the tops of the ripples in the walls and other hidden sources. The effect is extraordinary and deeply moving. Here, Dieste created the powerful effects of Baroque design for the modern age, and on a shoestring.

And, he did this time and again, not for resort hotels, ambitious museums or corporate headquarters, but for bus stations, food markets, warehouses, farm buildings, train depots and schools. An engineer in love with form, he used low-cost and often very cheap bricks to shape innovative vaults – unsupported over 50 metres (164 feet) and more, and lightweight in construction – and other structures that offered the poorest people and towns the most imaginative and uplifting architecture.

None of his experimentation was gratuitous. He spoke of structural 'resistance through form', meaning that the fecund forms he created were hard-working, practical or functional designs, and not forms for form's sake. What he questioned throughout his career was what was meant by purpose or function.

I climbed the perforated, cone-like bell tower of Christ the Worker. Only later, I read what Dieste had written about it some years before: 'A bell tower is, of course, made to hold bells, but it is also for lovers to climb on Sundays to view the landscape, for children to playing inside to relive the stories of long ago which lie asleep in all of us, to measure space, [and] above all when at each new spring swallows dart around it like living arrows.'

Today, a whole new generation of Latin American architects is working hard to build innovatively for the continent's teeming poor. The tendency is to eschew and downplay form and art, as if the poor deserve no more than basic – if decent and well-intentioned – shelter. Dieste, who died in 2000, showed it was possible to build poetically, using the cheapest materials, mathematical skill, structural wizardry and a true empathy for the dreams of ordinary people, for whom the extraordinary can make everyday life worthwhile and as special as it should be.

Zaha Hadid
Considerable or wayward talent?

The volcanic energy of Zaha Hadid's architectural office and design studio, and the sheer number of vivid buildings she and her multinational team – based in a red-brick Victorian Gothic former school in London – have realized around the world in just 20 years are phenomena of our times.

Along with buildings, Hadid (born in Baghdad, 1950, died in Miami, 2016) designed an outpouring of furniture, shoes, jewellery, ceramics and set designs. 'For an architect', she once told me, 'everything connects. The design of a handbag, or furniture or cutlery have their challenges, and they're fun to do. I'd love to get some designs into mass, low-cost production. I want to be able to touch everyone, not just the educated and cultural elite, with a little of what we can do. One of the things I feel confident in saying we can do is bring some excitement, and challenges, to people's lives. We want them to be able to embrace the unexpected.'

Famous, she was treated like a diva almost everywhere she went. Famous, she was offered one scheme after another for grand civic and

Swirling, sensuous interior of the auditorium, Heydar Aliyev Centre, Baku

commercial monuments, from Cincinnati through central Europe, central Asia and China. These rise in soaring, swooping forms, wild ideas made possible with computer programs and a tenacity that marked Hadid out from the beginning of her career.

This tenaciousness was a part of Hadid's character, but stems, too, from the way in which it was so hard for her to get going as an architect. A star from her days as a student and then teacher at London's Architectural Association School of Architecture, her talent was obvious, her paintings – influenced by Kazimir Malevich and the Russian Suprematists – as energetic as they were compelling. In 1994, she won a competition to design a particularly fine opera house on Cardiff Bay. It was rejected by the Millennium Commission, the project's financial backer, on grounds of unspecified 'uncertainties' (i.e. philistinism, chauvinism and xenophobia). Hadid's confidence was rocked. But, the year before, she had completed a dramatic fire station for the Vitra furniture factory at Weil am Rein on the Swiss-German border. It was to make her name as an architect.

If the British were not convinced by Hadid (an Iraqi, a woman and, nominally, a Muslim), Europeans were. Commissions followed, from the Austrian Ski Federation (Bergisel Ski Jump, Innsbruck, 2002), BMW (BMW Central Building, Leipzig, 2005) and the City of Wolfsburg (Phaeno Science Centre, 2005). The Rosenthal Center for Contemporary Arts (Cincinatti, 2003) established her name in the United States, while Rome took her up on her daring design for MAXXI, the National Museum of the XXI Century Arts, a project that spanned 12 years and finally opened to great acclaim in 2010.

For certain critics and fellow professionals, jealous, perhaps, of Hadid's seemingly sudden rise into the architectural firmament, it was soon time to go on the attack. This was made all the easier by Hadid's acceptance of commissions like the sensational Heydar Aliyev Center (2012) in Baku, Azerbaijan, a glorious building for a less-than-glorious political regime, although who is to say Italian Renaissance cities were any better? Of her work on this, the British architect Sean Griffiths said, 'It's basically an empty vessel that sucks in whatever ideology might be in proximity to it. In Moscow in 1923 it might have been interesting ...'

Bergisel Ski Jump, Innsbruck, Austria

Hadid told me, in an interview for *the Guardian* in 2006, 'I started out trying to create buildings that would sparkle like isolated jewels; now I want them to connect, to form a new kind of landscape, to flow together with contemporary cities and the lives of their peoples. What I would really love to build are schools, hospitals, social housing. Of course I believe imaginative architecture can make a difference to people's lives, but I wish it was possible to divert some of the effort we put into ambitious museums and galleries into the basic architectural building blocks of society.'

Architects, though, can only build what they are asked to. From the 1980s, the global shift from social to commercial ideals, from society to the individual, from industry to making money has meant it has been hard for architects to engage with projects that form the basic building blocks of everyday life.

'We were without work for so long', Hadid told me, 'that I haven't lost the habit of saying yes to every job. Call this insecurity if you like. I'm aware that we could slip into a slick mass-production mode, but I don't think we will. Maybe, though, I'll have to start saying no.' This, however, was always very unlikely.

One day, perhaps, the nature of architectural commissions will change and this 'planet in her own inimitable orbit', as the Dutch architect Rem Koolhaas has described his former student, might have come down to earth to work on more humble commissions. But it was not to be. Hadid's life was cut short. Her remarkable architecture should be enjoyed for its own sake.

St Petersburg
Neoclassical Arcadia or Tsarist Hades?

During the Great Northern War (1700–21), when Russia and her allies thwarted the seemingly unstoppable territorial ambitions of Sweden during the dashing, if reckless, reign of Charles XII, Peter the Great seized a stretch of land on the Gulf of Finland, allowing him to build Russia's first year-round seaport.

Founded with the building of a fortress in 1703, this was named St Petersburg. It was to be the world's most northerly city at the time of its completion. But far from just setting geographical records and giving Peter ready access to the Baltic, St Petersburg was to become, by decree, the new Russian capital, a modern city laid out and designed in the latest French and Italian manner, initially by the Swiss-Italian architect Domenico Trezzini, who established Russia's first school of architecture, and then by Peter's first Architect General, Jean-Baptiste Alexandre Le Blond, a Parisian noted for his landscaped gardens as well as for his buildings. In 1716, Le Bond drew up plans for standardized buildings for St Petersburg: the Tsar wanted order as well as beauty.

A St Petersburg street along a canal, modelled on Venice

The indefatigable Peter built as fast as it was possible to in this land of floods, mosquitoes, malaria and climatic extremes. A summer temperature of 37.1°C (98.8°F) has been recorded. In 1883 this fell to -35.9°C (-32.6°F). No one knows quite how many hundreds of thousands of Russian serfs and Swedish prisoners of war died to build St Petersburg. There is no doubt, though, that this most ambitious of cities was shaped from an unholy trinity of suffering, disease and premature death. Like a curse, this deathly birth pervaded the spirit of the place. As Fyodor Dostoevksy, one of the city's most famous sons, wrote in *Crime and Punishment* (1866), 'This is a city of half-crazy people ... there are few places where you'll find so many gloomy, harsh and strange influences on the soul of a man as in St Petersburg.'

And yet, from a purely visual consideration, St Petersburg was also one of the most beautiful cities the world had ever seen. Regulations that kept the height of buildings in check and refused idle and

Winter Square, looking towards the great sweep of Carlo Rossi's General Staff Building

unsightly spaces between city buildings, shaped harmonious streets and boulevards. This order was happily offset by the exuberance of facades, and the bright colours of many buildings, their apparent cheerfulness reflected in the waters of Venetian-style canals.

For all this careful planning and classical beauty, St Petersburg was to remain an unsettled city. It has changed its name three times (Petrograd, 1914; Leningrad, 1924; St Petersburg, again, 1991). It has been subject to Stalin's purges and to the terrible 872-day German siege of 1941–44, when around a million citizens died, most from starvation. Today, contempt for the city is rife. From 2005, demolition of historic buildings has been permitted. Crude high-rise buildings and blatantly bling skyscrapers are destroying the integrity of the Neoclassical skyline. Business before beauty. Corruption in place of civility. The threat of polonium tea for protestors. It is a sorry state of affairs, but then St Petersburg rises on a gulf of infinite sadness.

High Tech

Boy's Own adventure or revolutionary style for our times?

High Tech is a style or, more properly, an approach to architecture associated since the 1970s principally with the work of Norman Foster, Richard Rogers and Renzo Piano. A fascination with new materials, lightweight structures, the ideas of Buckminster Fuller, *Dan Dare: Pilot of the Future*, prefabrication, NASA and the elegance of engineering design – from Paxton's Crystal Palace to the latest polycarbonate sailplanes – gelled, one way or other, in these and other architects' minds.

Banking hall atrium of Norman Foster's HSBC, Hong Kong

What they shaped in a very short period was a sensation of buildings – notably, the Pompidou Centre (Piano and Rogers, 1977), the Hong Kong & Shanghai Bank headquarters (Foster Associates, 1986), the Lloyd's Building, London (Richard Rogers Partnership, 1986) – that gave a new burst of energy to Modern architecture and the debate surrounding its future.

What these buildings had in common was a heightened form of structural expression. Their method of construction, their structural engineering was made manifest. With its services on the outside of the building, painted red and blue, the Pompidou Centre did indeed have something of the look of a factory or oil refinery, yet it was also exuberant and generous, a building for both visitors and curators to enjoy and play with.

Rogers and co played a similar game with Lloyd's of London. Here the exposed services, including glass lifts shooting up the outside of the building, allowed the architects to create a soaring atrium inside, an appropriate space for this extremely busy City of London insurance market, and one of London's most exhilarating interiors.

Foster's designs have been cooler, sleeker and more collected: airliners to Rogers's oil rigs. Both architects, when students together at Yale, had travelled across the United States to look at the latest architecture. In California, they were thrilled not only by the enticing Case Study Houses – modern sonnets in steel and glass by, among others, Craig Ellwood and Pierre Koenig – but also by the Schools Construction Systems Development (SCSD) project, a 'High-Tech' building system launched in 1962, making extensive use of prefabricated lightweight space frames and serviced ceilings to create flexible space within low-cost buildings. The system was employed in dozens of overcrowded Californian schools. The project architect, Ezra Ehrenkrantz (1932–2001), was a contemporary of Foster and Rogers. They learned much from him.

Although many of their later buildings were big and ambitious, these High-Tech architects retained their fascination with lightness, with 'doing more with less', as Buckminster Fuller, who worked with Foster in London in the 1980s, put it. They have also kept faith with the idea of benign technological progress, believing that architecture can be both environmentally aware and as supra-modern as a Saturn V space rocket seemed when Foster, Rogers, Piano and others launched themselves into the architectural stratosphere in the mid-1960s.

Brutalism
Grim or lovable concrete?

Brutalism is something of a catch-all label for architecture of the 1950s to '70s making an overt or ostentatious use of rough (French *brut* or 'raw') concrete. It is a style, of sorts, encompassing legions of tough-looking buildings – notably town halls, university teaching blocks, theatres, concert halls, shopping centres and municipal car parks – found anywhere from the former Soviet republics of central Asia to Caracas (the city's Teresa Carreño Cultural Complex, opened in 1983, is a gem of sorts) via London, Plymouth and Boston, Massachusetts.

The origins of the term seem comic today. The Swedish architect Hans Asplund applied the label *nybrutalism* ('new brutalism') to a polite brick house in Uppsala, designed by his contemporaries Bengt Edman and Lennart Holm. What matters to the story of Brutalism is that Asplund's joke (I assume it was a joke) was picked up by visiting British architects, then very much under the spell of Scandinavian design, and repeated in print by the critic Reyner Banham.

Just as curiously, Banham, then working for the *Architectural Review*, applied the term in turn to a new school at Hunstanton on the north Norfolk coast by Alison and Peter Smithson. If anything, this much-photographed building owed more to Mies van der Rohe than to anything Scandinavian. In any case, it made little visible use of concrete, refined or raw.

Ah yes, but the idea was that a Brutalist building was one that, like Hunstanton, made explicit and raw use of materials. This was hardly convincing either. And yet, most of us have an image of a Brutalist building in mind. No, not Le Corbusier's magnificent Unité d'Habitation housing block in Marseilles, but London's Hayward Gallery (1968) and Queen Elizabeth Hall (1967) at the South Bank Centre, or Ernö Goldfinger's Trellick Tower (1972) looming over Portobello Road. Or Boston City Hall (1968), or – and tellingly – the Normandy coast defences built by the Todt Organisation to defend Nazi-occupied Europe from the Allied invasion that finally came in June 1944. Or, such peculiar, if utterly fascinating, buildings as the church of Sainte-Bernadette du Banlay, Nevers (1966), by Claude Parent and Paul Virilio, which is, unapologetically, a newly built Atlantic gun emplacement reimagined as a cave-like Catholic church, as far away from the ocean as it is possible to get in France. Parent and Virilio called this 'Oblique architecture' and not Brutalism. Whatever it is, in 2000 this challenging church was declared a national historic monument.

Much to their frustration, architects who made a considered use of concrete in the 1960s and '70s, like Denys Lasdun, architect of the Royal National Theatre, London, were labelled 'Brutalists'. I lived in the Barbican Estate in the City of London for four years. Well made – the 'raw' concrete effect had been realized by Italian craftsmen – with an abundance of lovingly tended window boxes and stepped Indian-style water gardens, and meticulously maintained, it seemed as brutal as a summer tea party in a vicarage garden. And yet, it has been labelled 'Brutalist' time and again. But then, even Sir John Vanbrugh has been described as a 'proto-brutalist'. Rather delightfully, the sculpted skylines of the three tall residential towers of the Barbican Estate owe very much to Vanbrugh. They are playful, not brutal.

The appeal of this loose-fit movement or style lies, I think, in the way that it is defiantly different. It cocks a snook at the conventions of crisp and polite architectural styles. It appeals, as punk rock did to public schoolboys, to those who would like architecture to be just a little foul-mouthed at times. Unlike, of course, Bengt Edman and Lennart Holm's charming villa in Uppsala.

Teresa Carreño Cultural Complex, Caracas

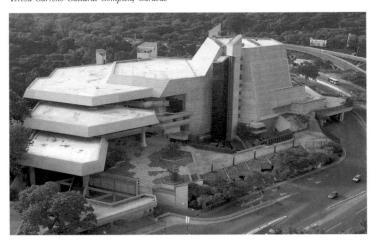

The Car

Liberator of citizens,
or conqueror of cities?

'I will build a motor car for the great multitude ... constructed of the best materials, by the best men to be hired, after the simplest designs that modern engineering can devise ... so low in price that no man making a good salary will be unable to own one, and enjoy with his family the blessing of hours of pleasure in God's great open spaces.'

This was Henry Ford speaking in 1913. He was, of course, as good as his word. Between 1908 and 1927, the Ford Motor Company manufactured and mass-produced 15 million Model Ts. It was the company's only model. It put the United States behind the driving wheel, opened up the highways and byways of the continent, and revolutionized life not just out in God's great open spaces but towns and cities, too.

The problem, though, unforeseen by Ford, a farm boy by birth, was congestion. Towns and cities, and the roads leading into, out of and around them, became clogged with cars. What could be done

Rooftop of the Fiat Lingotto factory, Turin, in the 1930s

about this? Why not build fast-flowing freeways through cities, on stilts and through buildings if need be? For decades the idea that the car was king and took precedence over pedestrians, sidewalks and the historic city centres held sway like some religious dogma.

Anyone who took against the car was a reactionary or dangerous conservationist, probably a communist, although they loved cars, too. Even Lenin, the dictator of the proletariat, owned two Rolls-Royces to drive around his worker's paradise. Along with congestion, the car marred the appearance of streets and buildings, although it has given rise to such exciting buildings as the Futurist-inspired Fiat Lingotto factory in Turin (1923), and such eye-boggling designs as Bertrand Goldberg's Marina City, Chicago (1964). The first 19 floors of the Marina's twin 65-storey towers, styled unwittingly or not in the guise of giant corn cobs, are car parks winding tightly around the central core of the towers. After dark they are a source of cinematic pleasure as headlamps flash up and around the concrete cobs.

When the car was finally banned from 'pedestrian only' city zones, these often proved to be listless places devoid of the energy and excitement traffic brings with it. This was a conundrum. The car offered freedom, yet brought visual blight, congestion, pollution, frayed tempers and new taxes to towns and cities. It might go altogether one day, yet I, for one, am rather sorry I was unable to buy Colonel Richard Seifert's 1967 Jensen FF when it came up for sale in 2010. This controversial London architect ordered the car on completion of Centre Point Tower, the fashion-model thin skyscraper his firm had designed and negotiated through the city's planning system for the developer Harry Hyams, who himself bought a pair of FFs. His wife won a third at a charity dinner.

If the story of Centre Point Tower is not exactly edifying, the Jensen is a very special car. Many architects love their cars, and even collect them, yet feel the need to run them down in public. Every twenty-first-century architecture project has to be 'sustainable'. The car is unsustainable. Henry Ford left us with a conundrum we have yet to solve.

Parametric Design
Computer-game fad, or a lasting new future for architecture?

Parametric design became an intensely fashionable process in the twenty-first century, as if it had never existed before. Essentially what it means is that the relationship between elements or the structural components of a building can be manipulated, usually through computer programs, to inform and create new and complex geometries. This allows buildings to spring up in remarkable twists and turns, as if unrestrained by the conventions of structure, materials and design itself.

Not surprisingly, perhaps, the major treatise on the subject can be found in two weighty volumes (*The Autopoiesis of Architecture*, 2010) by Patrik Schumacher, director and senior designer with Zaha Hadid Architects. This practice has made its reputation with the design of some of the most adventurous buildings of modern times. Schumacher discusses how various modes of communication comprising architecture depend upon each other, combine, and form a unique subsystem of society that co-evolves with other important autopoietic (self-producing) subsystems like art, science, politics and the economy. In other words, Schumacher has attempted to create a unifying theory of architecture lending theoretical support to his practice's work. Parametric design allows architecture to push forward into the territory of autopoiesis.

In the wrong hands – and wrong computer programs – and without such intellectual underpinning, the parametric design process has allowed architects to play madcap games with the shape of buildings. Changes can be made for change's sake, and so we have had to learn to walk through cities decorated as if by a troop of drunken baboons with buildings that bend, twist, writhe and lean to no artistic effect.

Zaha Hadid showed how parametric design and art can coalesce to exquisite kinetic effect in an installation, *Parametric Space*, she created in collaboration with Danish design studio Kollision, research studio CAVI and motion designers Wahlberg, for the Danish Architecture Centre, Copenhagen, in 2013.

Intriguingly, parametric design itself predates computers. In the Sagrada Família Museum, beneath the Passion Facade of this ambitious basilica (see page 30), you can see a model made by Antoni Gaudí of his church at Colonia Güell on the industrial outskirts of Barcelona. This upside-down model demonstrates how Gaudí designed the complex vault, the like of which had never been seen before. Strings of various lengths hanging from the top of the model and weighted with birdshot were adjusted to vary the shape of the vaults. Gaudí used a mirror to look up inside the model to see how its parameters changed as the length and positions of the strings were adjusted.

Computers have replaced such models, yet it worked: parametric design a century ago. The church for the Colonia Güell, however, was never remotely completed. What you see today is the lower of what were to have been two naves, one on top of the other, topped by towers of different heights between a central dome. Perhaps it was wise to have put an end to the project. Parametricism can indeed be a design too far.

Hazza Bin Zayed Stadium, United Arab Emirates, by Pattern Design

Victorian Gothic
Nineteenth-century romance or vulgar blight?

Ten days before demolition was due to begin in November 1967, St Pancras Chambers, until 1935 a grandiloquent Victorian hotel, and the railway terminus behind this extreme Gothic Revival extravaganza, were listed Grade I, ensuring, at the very least, that they would survive. The plan had been to replace this peerless architectural ensemble with a glum new sports centre, an office block and soulless housing.

In November 2007, the Queen reopened St Pancras, now superbly restored not just as a grand hotel and rooftop flats for the well-to-do, but as a railway station of great complexity, providing services around London, across London and all the way to Paris by a new high-speed link ingeniously engineered under the city.

The campaign to save St Pancras, led by the poet, journalist and architectural historian John Betjeman, had occupied five long and acrimonious years. It had not been simply a case of working hard to persuade the public at large and fellow architectural historians that

Keble College Chapel, Oxford

St Pancras was worth saving, for while the value of Sir Giles Gilbert Scott's magnificent Midland Grand Hotel and William Barlow and Rowland Ordish's sublime train shed seem blindingly obvious today, this was not so in 1967.

John Summerson, Britain's pre-eminent architectural historian at the time, continued to look down his long nose at St Pancras. In 1968 he was still bemoaning the 'disintegration of architecture and engineering' between Scott's hotel and Barlow's train shed. Summerson sniffed at the 'total separation of functional and "artistic" criteria in separate heads and hands'. How odd. Had he never raised his eyes to the high peak of Barlow and Ordish's great arch and realized that this was a Gothic design, too, a pitch-perfect engineering foil to the architect's 'artistic' hotel?

What I think Summerson, contemporary British Railways' executives and all too many politicians of the mid-60s disliked about St Pancras is that it reminded them of their antiquated upbringing, all strict nannies, ice-cold bedrooms, improving books, excessive corporal punishment and morning doses of cod liver oil. This generation wanted to be staunchly modern, not starchily Victorian or even extravagantly Edwardian.

While it is true that Victorian Gothic buildings do seem wild set alongside their graceful Georgian predecessors, they are often romantic and exciting designs. And, yet, can we ever really learn to love such extreme Victorian designs as William Butterfield's Keble College, Oxford, or George Gilbert Scott Jr's terrifying Cathedral Church of St John the Baptist on Unthank Road, Norwich? It was, though, the soaring vaults and ambitious interior spaces of Alfred Waterhouse's Manchester Town Hall that first encouraged Norman Foster, a supreme Modernist, to think of becoming an architect.

The Victorians built an awful lot – especially churches – in a vain attempt to make industrial Britain somehow spiritual. So there are hundreds of rather plodding or else overwrought Victorian Gothic buildings, yet they nearly always deserve a second look. By failing to look carefully, the world, and not just London, very nearly lost St Pancras, among the very best of challenging Victorian Gothic designs.

Sydney Opera House
Symbol of altruism or pettiness?

'The drawings submitted for this scheme are simple to the point of being diagrammatic. Nevertheless, as we have returned again and again to the study of these drawings, we are convinced that they present a concept of an Opera House which is capable of becoming one of the great buildings of the world ... because of its very originality, it is clearly a controversial design. We are, however, absolutely convinced of its merits.'

These are the prescient words of the four-man judging panel, including Eero Saarinen, which, in January 1957 chose 39-year old Jørn Utzon, a glamorous if largely untested Danish architect, to design the Sydney Opera House. Fifty years later, the building, opened in 1973, was declared a Unesco World Heritage Site. The expert report to the World Heritage Committee stated, 'it stands by itself as one of the indisputable masterpieces of human creativity, not only in the twentieth century but in the history of humankind.'

Such sentiments had cut no ice with Davis Hughes, the new Minister for Public Works appointed in 1965 after the success of the

Sketch by Jørn Utzon of outline design, 1957

Liberals in the New South Wales election. The Opera House had been a Labour project, and an expensive one, too. As Elizabeth Farrelly, the Australian architect and critic noted in a brilliant *Sydney Morning Herald* obituary of Utzon (1 December 2008), 'At an election night dinner party in Mosman, Hughes's daughter, Sue Burgoyne, boasted that her father would soon sack Utzon. Hughes had no interest in art, architecture or aesthetics. A fraud, as well as a philistine, he had been exposed before Parliament and dumped as Country Party leader for 19 years of falsely claiming a university degree. The Opera House gave Hughes a second chance. For him, as for Utzon, it was all about control; about the triumph of homegrown mediocrity over foreign genius.'

Australia's relationship with the avant-garde, Farrelly added, had always been timid. Australians were curious but mistrustful; interested but deeply risk-averse. They were frightened. And mid-century Sydney, immortally described by one reviewer as 'King George's gulag', was the epicentre of this timidity. Australia's tectonic shift into the modern world was belated, and all the more violent for it. It was this clash of forces – primal fear versus euphoric optimism – in which Utzon found himself trapped.

Utzon's was a quixotic talent, and yet it was philistinism and spite on Hughes's part that saw the architect's unpaid fees rise to

The illuminated Opera House with Sydney Harbour Bridge behind

$100,000 by February 1966. Not surprisingly, he quit, and went to live in a beautiful, elemental house of his own design (he and his wife, Lis, put me up there for several days in the mid-1980s), overlooking the sea in Majorca. After Sydney, he rarely built again. When the Opera House opened, Utzon, in a gesture of reconciliation, was awarded the Australian Institute of Architects' Gold Medal. He neither attended the royal opening nor left Majorca to receive the medal. When he died, I wrote of my own first trip to Sydney in the *Guardian*:

'Walking on the roof on the Sydney Opera House lit up by a full moon on my first trip to Australia remains one of my cherished Utzon moments. It was wonderful to think, if dreamily, that the great, sail-like roofs all around me, framing kaleidoscopic views of the harbourside city, might be pieced together by some giant hand to form a perfect sphere. Here was geometric ingenuity, technical wizardry and sheer architectural sorcery: the poetics of space. Both Gaudí and Le Corbusier would have applauded. Dumbfounded, I was unable to make even that simple, universal gesture.'

In April 2003, it was announced that Utzon was to receive the Pritzker Architecture Prize. The citation read, 'There is no doubt that the Sydney Opera House is his masterpiece. It is one of the great iconic buildings of the twentieth century, an image of great beauty that has become known throughout the world – a symbol for not only a city, but a whole country and continent.'

David Hughes died the month before, although it is not difficult to imagine his response. 'Stone the crows. That project was like a mad woman's breakfast and the foreign fella who designed it struck me as having a few kangaroos loose in the top paddock.' Hughes was knighted in 1975.

Shaker Style
Design for life or death?

The very last active Shaker community can be found at Sabbathday Lake, Maine. The last time I checked, there were three members. There had been 20 settlements and 6,000 Shakers in the mid-nineteenth century, but as these members of the United Society of Believers in Christ's Second Appearing are strictly celibate, their numbers have steadily dwindled as vocations have dried up, too.

There is something strangely lifeless in beautiful settlements like Hancock Shaker Village, Massachusetts, run as a museum today. The eighteenth-century-style buildings – plain, simple and perfectly proportioned – are unquestionably beautiful. Shaker design – plain, simple and perfectly proportioned chairs and benches – is enchanting and is a feature of thousands of educated middle-class homes around the world. But, the Shakers themselves are missing. No amount of well-intended curating can replace their way of life and their dissenting religious beliefs and famous dances, 'shaking' for Christ rather than with Elvis. Shaker architecture is soulful, but the life that made it has all but gone. It speaks of the tomb far more than it does the cradle.

Office interior at Hancock Shaker Village, Pittsfield, Massachusetts

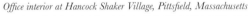

Outrage
Valiant or pointless campaign?

Ian Nairn joined the *Architectural Review* from the RAF, where he had flown Gloster Meteor fighter jets. His pilot's view had allowed him to plot something of the sprawl snaking out from and encompassing English towns and cities. He made his mark instantly, with a special issue of the magazine – 'Outrage' – published in 1955. This was based on a drive the 25-year-old had made in his soft-top Morris Minor from the Solent in the south to the River Eden in the north. He forged a word for what he saw on what was then a long trip by congested A-roads: Subtopia.

'Its symptoms will be', he wrote, 'that the end of Southampton will look like the beginning of Carlisle; the parts in between will look like the end of Carlisle or the beginning of Southampton.' And the outrage? 'The Outrage is that the whole land surface is becoming covered by the creeping mildew that already circumscribes all of our towns … Subtopia is the annihilation of the site, the steamrollering of all individuality of place to one uniform and mediocre pattern.'

This could have been William Cobbett riding his hobby horse across southern England: 'All Middlesex is ugly', he thundered in 1830 in one of the pugnacious chapter openings of *Rural Rides*. Much the same theme was taken up by John Ruskin, John Betjeman, the architect Clough Williams-Ellis, who gave us Portmeirion in north Wales, and Thomas Sharp, a twentieth-century town planner who believed that post-war Modern architecture and development could be reconciled with the humane ideal – felt by Nairn in the bones of his burly frame – of compact towns co-existing with a truly green countryside of which we are stewards, not consumers or despoilers.

Nairn battled on in the specialist and national press, in books and on television. But, despite so many weasel words by politicians and bureaucrats, placemen and, in recent years, think tanks and quangos, Subtopia has spread far further than even Nairn might have imagined in his most gothic nightmares. Sixty years on from when we first heard his distinctive voice, we should be more outraged than ever. Subtopia rules much of the world. Ian Nairn drank himself to an early death.

Cover of Outrage *edition of the* Architectural Review, *1955*

Albert Kahn
American hero or Soviet stooge?

To date, and in purely quantitative terms, Albert Kahn (1869–1942) must surely be the world's greatest architect. The son of a Prussian Rabbi who emigrated with his family to Detroit in 1880, and with little formal education, Kahn's career was meteoric. A pioneer of wide-span reinforced concrete structures, his Packard factory design of 1903 caught the eye of Henry Ford for whom Kahn was to design more than 1,000 projects, including the Highland Park Plant of 1910. This is where Ford perfected his mass-production assembly line. Kahn went on to design the masterplan (1917) and several key buildings of the Ford River Rouge Complex, Dearborn, the world's largest integrated production plant.

In 1929, Kahn was asked to design the ambitious Stalingrad Tractor Plant. The Soviets, lacking such talent, were hugely

B-24 bombers at the Willow Run mile-long assembly plant

impressed by what Ford and Kahn had achieved to such great effect in so little time. The plant went on to build thousands of potent and reliable T-34 tanks during World War II. Kahn was rewarded with a commission to consult on all factories rushed up at Stakhanovite speed during the USSR's first two Five-Year Plans. He built more than 500 factories, training some 4,000 Soviet architects and engineers in the process.

Back in the USA, and by the late 1930s, Kahn employed 600 architects. The practice designed a fifth of all US manufacturing plants. His half-million-dollar salary was one of the highest in the country. 'Architecture', he said, 'is 90 per cent business and ten per cent art.'

With the outbreak of the World War II, Kahn's special kind of genius paid dividends over and again. The design of his massive Detroit Arsenal Tank Plant, established in Warren, Michigan by Chrysler in 1940 for the mass production of military tanks, allowed these to roll off the production line even before the building was properly completed. A quarter of all US tanks were produced here between 1941 and 1945. The bombproof building was designed to be put to civilian uses after hostilities ceased, and though this has come to pass in part, a large section of this massive structure remains in use by the military today.

Kahn's last project was the Willow Run bomber plant, Michigan (1941), for the mass production of Consolidated B-24 Liberator bombers by the Ford Motor Company. The assembly line was a mile long, very probably the world's largest space under a single roof.

If Kahn had built nothing other than these hugely impressive US and Soviet factories, his reputation would have stood high, although there must have been some at least in the States who found it odd, and even wrong, that a professional from the land of the capitalist free should work so hard for the darn Commies, with their plot to take over the world. Kahn, though, built far more. Art Deco skyscrapers, Shingle-style houses, Neoclassical university halls and graceful parkland conservatories. These and other designs were raced off with great aplomb by one of the most productive architectural practices ever known.

Adolf Loos
Hovering on genius or insanity?

What on earth would Adolf Loos (1870–1933) have made of life in the twenty-first century, when what appears to be 90 per cent of the population sports tattoos and is dressed in the barest of clothes, covered in random messages and artless decoration?

In 1908, at the height of the lush Art Nouveau and Vienna Secession movements, Loos, a largely self-taught architect – born the son of a German stonemason in Brunn, Moravia – wrote *Ornament and Crime*, a provocative essay charting the progress of human culture in proportion to a decline in decoration. If a man of the new twentieth century were to tattoo himself like a Papuan, Loos argued, we would consider him to be degenerate, and even criminal. The architect went so far as to sketch the tattooed criminals in Viennese prisons. 'No ornament', wrote Loos, 'can any longer be made today by anyone who lives on our cultural level … freedom from ornament is a sign of spiritual strength.'

Loos went on to design elegant and restrained villas, shops and a famous bar (the Kärtner in Vienna, better known today as the American Bar) for sophisticated and wealthy clients in the Austro-Hungarian capital, in Pilsner and in Prague. His refined interiors, although free of decoration, were fashioned in rich and luxurious materials. They are not exactly precursors of the Modern Movement, as a number of twentieth-century architectural historians worked hard to prove, but they are refined designs from the mind of a perfectionist.

Loos was a challenging figure. He had three tumultuous marriages, was brought to court in 1928 for dalliances with underage girls, and showed early signs of dementia. Oh dear. And yet, who is to say Loos was wrong about adornment? Today, insane mass consumerism and the wilful dumbing down of culture has indeed gone ink-on-skin with the mass popularization of tattooing and the decorating of towns and cities with shopping malls and laugh-out-loud new museums. Like all true controversialists, Loos makes awkward reading, now as then. The brilliance of his buildings, however, remains a joy for everyone to share.

The American Bar, Vienna

Philip Johnson
An architect for every occasion,
or New York hooker?

How many times did Philip Johnson (1906–2005), a highly intelligent and equally controversial American architect, make the connection between architecture and prostitution? 'Architects are pretty much high-class whores. We can turn down projects the way they can turn down some clients, but we've both got to say yes to someone if we want to stay in business.' I do not know when or where Johnson said this, although in a talk he gave at the Graham Foundation, Chicago, on 15 December 1972, he said, 'Like good prostitutes, we do our stuff when we are paid. We try to do it well for whoever will pay.'

Did the waspish Johnson protest too much? No. Here was a wealthy and cultured man who came late to architecture, graduating when he was 37, and who changed his style and approach like a model changing costumes for a fashion show. In the early 1930s he was a keen 'white' Modernist, introducing the US public to Le Corbusier, Mies van der Rohe and Walter Gropius at the 'International Style'

Serene interior of Johnson's Glass House

show he put on at the New York Museum of Modern Art with the historian Henry-Russell Hitchcock.

Johnson also joined an American Nazi party, attending at least one Nuremberg rally to hear Hitler speak and, as if Mel Brooks was writing for him, reported the German invasion of Poland for US Nazis in 1939. 'The German green uniforms made the place look gay and happy. There were not many Jews to be seen. We saw Warsaw burn and Modlin being burned. It was a stirring spectacle.'

Post-war, he was a good Mid-Century Modern – his remarkably modest and beautifully realized Glass House of 1949 on his Connecticut estate is his finest work, along with the lobby of Mies's Seagram Building on Park Avenue – and then, finding less a bore, he became an arch Postmodernist, producing one giant office scheme after another with his partner John Burgee, in any style any oil tycoon or business corporation could be hooked with: neo-neo-Gothic in Pittsburgh, split-pedimented 'Chippendale' in Manhattan.

He later championed Deconstructivism, enjoying his role as US style monger-in-chief. For Johnson, architecture was about art and style, making money and being taken note of. He certainly made a noise, although he died peacefully in his sleep in the Glass House. Perhaps he just wanted to be loved.

Philip Johnson outside the Glass House

Arts and Crafts
Noble rusticity, or Morris dancing for architects?

The English Arts and Crafts movement – a style and, equally perhaps, a moral crusade – flourished between 1880 and 1910. The houses its leading practitioners crafted – Home Place, Holt, and the Barn, Exmouth, by E. S. Prior; the Orchard, Chorleywood, by C. F. A. Voysey; and Stoneywell, Ulverscroft, by Ernest Gimson among them – are quietly exciting and, as anyone should expect, beautifully made things. Between them, they also embody a number of paradoxes.

Heartily promoted by William Morris (1834–96), a multi-talented and hugely energetic weaver, writer, artist and capitalist who championed communism, the Arts and Crafts movement was fuelled by an anti-industrial spirit. It dreamed, as Ruskin and Pugin had done, of reviving a world of content craftsmen, a Merrie England of sorts where everyone would live in harmony with nature, and every man (and woman, too) would be an artist, when not busy

The Orchard, Chorleywood, Hertfordshire

Morris dancing around the village maypole, modelling a smock or setting up a local folk song society.

From the start, the difficulty with this was clear. Beautiful tapestries, hand-printed books and well-turned oak chairs built of the very best traditional materials and designed down to the last nail were always going to be costly. Morris complained of his own 'ministering to the swinish luxury of the rich'. Arts and Crafts houses were for the well off, too. Morris's own Red House, Bexleyheath, a very early example from 1859 designed by Philip Webb, was a case in point. However modest it seemed in comparison with contemporary lush Victoriana, its fine materials and an interior furnished and burnished by Webb, Morris, his aesthetic wife Janey and the Pre-Raphaelite painter Edward Burne-Jones, made it an expensive proposition. Today, the Red House is surrounded by suburbia and houses crafted with as much care as a supermarket, yet styled – and here's the rub – on Arts and Crafts architecture.

Did Voysey, who lived long enough to watch swathes of Middlesex and Hertfordshire meadows and market gardens blighted by developers' houses sold for about twice the average national salary, ever look from the Orchard to the encroaching catalogue of semi-detached homes and make the visual connection?

Home Place, Holt, Norfolk

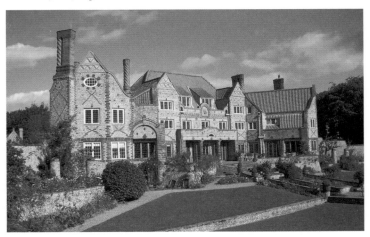

Charles Rennie Mackintosh
Great Scot or tourist attraction?

I have a confession to make, and one that no one reading this book could possibly understand. I have never been particularly keen on the work of Charles Rennie Mackintosh. The Glasgow School of Art, certainly, and, yes, the landscapes he painted in watercolour when living in Port Vendres in the south of France in the 1920s. But all that spindly furniture and those loopy white artistic interiors leave me cold.

My opinion, though, is wholly irrelevant to the Charles Rennie Mackintosh industry that has grown up in recent decades, and notably in Glasgow, a city that since World War II has done much to destroy its historic architecture. In Glasgow, you can find Mackintosh aprons and tea towels, coasters and cushions, plates and pendants, ties and wristwatches, key rings, postcards, cufflinks, teapots, brooches, trays, nightlights, whisky glasses, handbags and baseball caps, although, as yet, no raincoats. For the well heeled, reproductions of Mackintosh furniture are readily available from a variety of local and international sources.

The Glasgow School of Art

Well, if Barcelona trades off the reputation and architecture of Gaudí, why should Glasgow be in any way decried for cashing in on 'Toshie'? Like the architectural historian Gavin Stamp, I have a feeling that Glasgow's other great architect, Alexander 'Greek' Thomson (1817–75), remains, for all Stamp's pugnacious advocacy, underrated. When the necessary renovation of the Glasgow School of Art began soon after the fire that devastated the building in 2014, Thomson's stirring Egyptian Halls in Union Street remained in a state of dereliction, as they have done for the past 30 years.

Thomson designed magnificent commercial buildings and residential terraces for Glasgow, along with three wholly original and truly sublime churches, one destroyed by the Luftwaffe in the 1940s, another by local vandals in 1965. How odd to turn one local hero into a poster boy for the tourist industry and not the other. With luck and many prayers, more of Thomson's buildings will be saved in coming years, although if they are, perhaps we might just be spared 'Greek' Thomson tartans, triglyph T-shirts and fluted tumblers.

Refined interior of the House for an Art Lover, Glasgow

Architecture and Morality
Imperative or opportunism?

The idea that there is some distinctly moral dimension to architecture, not as in building well, but in terms of a right way of designing and building at a particular time, is a curious one. From the 1930s, however, the idea of morality and architecture was conflated with a very German notion, promulgated from the era of Georg Wilhelm Friedrich Hegel (1770–1831), of the zeitgeist, or 'spirit of the age'.

While there may or may not be such a spirit – life on earth, let alone the universe and what might exist beyond it, has never been less than a complex affair – a new generation of architectural historians, personified by Nikolaus Pevsner, a German scholar who found refuge in England thanks to Frank Pick, the design-minded and very moral chief executive of the London Passenger Transport Board, made a case that was frozen music to the ears of Modern Movement architects and their champions in the specialist press and publishing houses.

Cadmore Lane Junior School, Cheshunt, Hertfordshire, 1959

The twentieth-century zeitgeist was functionalism. A modern industrial society needed Modernism to shape its buildings, from factories to workers' houses, to their places of entertainment, edification and worship. It was the architect's duty to design in accordance with the zeitgeist. Not to do so was not simply to be old-fashioned or irrelevant, but immoral. To design in historic styles was anathema because this was not in keeping with the zeitgeist.

So, soulless, high-rise concrete estates and other drab functionalist buildings were philosophically and morally right. More than this, because Modernism had fulfilled the zeitgeist of the new society, architecture no longer needed historical styles. Modernism itself was not a style; it was a moral imperative. And so ...

I heard all this when I worked at the *Architectural Press* in Queen Anne's Gate, where old-fashioned patrician manners and an upper-crust English way of life went hand in hand with a hair-shirted Modernist radicalism. Post-war, prefabricated Hertfordshire schools good, Lutyens bad. Even Le Corbusier was questionable; from the mid-1940s he had moved into Expressionist territory, teetering on the immoral.

In 1977, David Watkin, a Cambridge historian, had published a thoughtful and provocative book, *Morality and Architecture*, demolishing the zeitgeist approach. At Queen Anne's Gate it was not a book you could admit to having read, let alone agreed with. The attempt to link morality to a particular era in terms of architecture has, however, long been a case of special pleading. Pugin did it to promote the revival of his beloved Gothic architecture. Ruskin did it, unconvincingly. Pevsner did it with zeal.

Modernism itself may indeed have been a creed, yet the architecture of the Modern Movement took on many forms. In the twenty-first century, the zeitgeist is money and aspiration, the new morality 'sustainability'. In practice this often means very little, yet architects repeat the word like a religious mantra, knowing they would be struck into the professional abyss if they failed to do so. Modern architects still need to appear to be moral.

Art Nouveau
Innovative artistry or frivolous conceit?

The 'New Art' that emerged across Europe and adopted several names – Art Nouveau, Jugendstil, Modernisme, Secession, Stile Liberty – flowered very briefly between 1895 and 1910, and yet this sensuous and self-consciously aesthetic movement – art for art's sake – continues to tease the imagination of writers, illustrators, film-makers, jewellers, interior decorators and fashion designers, if not architects, for whom, perhaps, it was altogether too flippant or fey.

Although there were major variations in the work of Art Nouveau architects – the serpentine entrances to the Paris Métro by Hector Guimard, the straight lines of Viennese Secessionism, the folkloric decorative elements found in Finland and Hungary – the underlying idea was that of the *Gesamtkunstwerk*, the all-embracing artwork, where every last detail of a building would be styled and crafted. Inevitably, this was an expensive business, and it is only rarely, as in Guimard's Métro entrances, the facades of fashionable city-centre cafes or in printed posters of works by the artist Henri Toulouse-Lautrec, for example, that Art Nouveau engaged with mass taste.

The style, although often enticing, with its serpentine lines, plant-like forms and writhing metalwork, was ensnared by the coils of Decadence, a movement of sorts that conflated Art Nouveau with the dreamy, absinthe-fuelled worlds of the late Pre-Raphaelites, Symbolist poets and painters, of Charles Baudelaire and Odilon Redon in Paris, and, in London, with Oscar Wilde, Aubrey Beardsley and Theodore Wratislaw, all drooping lilies, whiplash lines and dark sexuality.

Art Nouveau produced its masterpieces – it is hard not to be bowled over by the poised and sensual artistry of Victor Horta's Hôtel Tassel (1894) in Brussels, or to wander the streets of Katajanokka in Helsinki and not to admire the way in which Art Nouveau was used as a powerful and romantic symbol of burgeoning nationalism, and even employed in highly successful urban planning. I am not sure what Oscar or Bosie would have made of this. A bit too serious? Pass the absinthe dear boy. It will soon pass.

The Hôtel Tassel, Brussels

162

Concrete
Grim utility or rock bed of invention?

Concrete will not always be associated with stained, mildewed and grim high-rise local authority housing estates rushed up between the 1950s and 1970s, and yet the words 'concrete' and 'horror' are a close-knit pair in the English language.

The greatest 'concrete horror' of all was the Pruitt-Igoe housing project in St Louis, Missouri. Completed in 1956, it comprised 2,870 public housing apartments in 33 concrete slab blocks designed by Minoru Yamasaki (1912–86), architect of the ill-fated twin towers of the World Trade Center. Although residents considered their new homes an improvement on the slums many had come from, hustling by politicians and local authority departments, and haste in construction led to flaws that, combined with crime, poor maintenance, and an enforced policy of racial segregation, caused Pruitt-Igoe to fall from grace. Critic Charles Jencks commented 'Modern architecture died in St Louis, Missouri, on July 15, 1972 at 3.32pm … when the infamous Pruitt Igoe scheme, or rather several of its slab blocks, were given the final *coup de grâce* by dynamite.'

Playroom in the Pruitt-Igoe projects, St Louis, Missouri

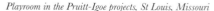

The death of Modern architecture has been exaggerated, and yet this apparent and large-scale failure of concrete was enough, in Jencks's view, to seal its fate. There is, of course, another side to the story of concrete and Modern architecture. The material has a noble history. Refined by the Romans, it had made such ambitious and enduring designs as the coffered dome over the Pantheon possible. It allowed the Romans to leap away, in vaults and bounds, from traditional trabeated (post and lintel) classical construction, as championed by the Greeks, and to shape the great public baths, basilicas, arenas and palaces we associate with their dynamic empire.

Modern forms of reinforced concrete have taken architecture into an adventure of new forms and scales. In the hands of Le Corbusier and his followers, it had been a moody, poetic material. In Japan, Tadao Ando (born 1941), a one-time boxer and lorry driver, has made concrete a thing of poised and pristine beauty.

With its malleable, plastic quality, great strength and low cost, concrete has allowed architects in the developing world to design and build with panache, and none more so than Oscar Niemeyer in Brazil (see page 52). There is poetry in concrete construction. It seems a pity that in their rush to build, using untried and untested materials and techniques, post-war politicians and their architects in Britain and the United States did such a disservice to the material.

Niemeyer's Brasília Cathedral, Brazil

United States Air Force Academy Chapel, Colorado Springs

Homage to God or to military?

'The Cadet Chapel staff's mission', says the United States Air Force, 'is to inspire men and women to become leaders of character through spiritual formation.' Many of these leaders of character will also fly some of the world's fastest and most potent military aircraft.

The scintillating Cadet Chapel at Colorado Springs fuses the spirit and technology of Jet Age fighters with an ethereal sense of spirituality. It is a truly remarkable structure, as striking today as it was when it opened for worship in 1962. It takes the form of 17 stainless steel spires – 46 metres (150 feet) high – in tight formation, composed of 100 tetrahedrons supported by concrete buttresses and rising like the upended swept wings of jet fighters from a concrete podium.

The narrow gaps between the spires are filled with mosaics of stained glass. Inside the nave – this is the Protestant chapel; chapels and prayer halls for other denominations, all of them special in their own way, are set beneath it – the effect is transcendental. This is one

Air Force Academy Chapel, Colorado Springs

of the world's most compelling and beautiful places of worship. Does this seem a little odd? Military parades, services and Mach 2 jets so close to divinity? And yet, cadets at Colorado Springs are required to recite 'High Flight', a favourite poem of pilots and astronauts around the world and into space. It was written by Pilot Officer John Gillespie Magee Jr (1922–41), a British-American Spitfire pilot, born in China, who signed up with the Royal Canadian Air Force to fight Hitler before the US joined the Allies. Magee's parents were Anglican missionaries. His father went on to become curate of St John's Evangelical Church, Washington, DC. Magee died when his Spitfire collided with another aircraft in Lincolnshire.

'High Flight' is not just his memorial, but that of all pilots. It is also one of the spiritual and architectural foundation stones of the Cadet Chapel at Colorado Springs. When I went to see the chapel's architect, Walter A. Netsch Jr (1920–2008) of SOM, Chicago, by then confined to a wheelchair, he recited it to me without hesitation.

Stained glass windows inside the nave of the Protestant chapel

Eco-towns
Green credentials, or greenwash?

In 2007, Britain's New Labour government announced a competition for the design of 15 'eco-towns'. From the beginning, the idea, if perhaps well intended, was potty. Controversial, too. The aim was to commission small 'zero carbon' new towns on green sites. Unlike traditional towns that need a purpose like trade, industry or even tourism to exist and thrive, eco-towns would be a good thing simply because they promised to use less energy than their predecessors.

The proposal seemed flawed from the outset. With few jobs in the offing, eco folk would need to use precious energy to commute to work in old towns. Critics from all walks of life

Idyllic representation of a future eco-town: monorail train glides over Butlin's holiday camp, Minehead, Somerset, 1967

viewed the competition with suspicion. Surely this was just a clever and fashionable way of getting around the slow grind of the British planning system in order to build lots of new homes on agricultural land.

In 2008, a proposal for one of the eco-towns at Hanley Grange, Cambridgeshire, was abandoned after Tesco, the supermarket giant, pulled out. Local people had dubbed it 'Tescotown'. It would have been centred on a large Tesco store with sustainable homes for Tesco staff and customers. This was scraping the barrel and everyone agreed, except for the New Labour government and its architectural advisors who, knowing that such development strips life and business from the high streets of old country towns, liked nothing better than to help promote big new superstores in the English countryside, especially Tesco, wherever and whenever they spotted an opportunity. Quite why they chose to do so remains a mystery.

Now, though, the game was up. Just one eco-town, North West Bicester – the first and last – started on site five years after this government think-tank sally was announced. It would have been far better, and ultimately more 'sustainable', to improve life and to build anew in existing country towns.

The problem with this particular eco-town project is that it was driven by public relations, vote-catching and greenwash – fashionable and even fatuous talk ('hot air') relating to environmental issues – rather than a genuine or properly thought through concern for the future of towns and buildings.

In other parts of Europe, the matter has been taken far more seriously. In Freiberg, Germany, for example, a town noted for its green initiatives, architects like Rolf Disch are proving that buildings – from homes to office blocks – can use minimal energy. The aim is not to win political points, but to think and build thoughtfully for all our futures.

Even then, traditional towns, and indeed ancient towns, remind us of how very many settlements and buildings were 'green' before the advent of modern technology, the car and environmentalism itself.

Dunmore Pineapple, Scotland
Costly self-indulgence, or investment in architectural delight?

'What do you think it cost to build?', a friend asked some years ago as we looked up from summer drinks to the sublime, if ever so slightly comic, 14-metre (45-foot) stone pineapple commanding the six-acre walled garden of Dunmore Park.

Without eighteenth-century records to hand, I had no idea. In any case, even if I had been able to put a figure on the cost, this would not have translated into any meaningful financial comparison with what we spend today on anything from cars and homes to holidays and digital gizmos. The Dunmore Pineapple was expensive, yet at the time architecture and landscape gardens were the thing to spend big money on, and follies, whatever their cost, have repaid us a hundred times over in terms of enduring delight.

The Dunmore Pineapple is one of Britain's finest architectural follies. Although the story has been muddled over the years, John Murray, 4th Earl of Dunmore, seems to have built it on his return

The Dunmore Pineapple, Stirlingshire

from America in 1777, where he had been the last British Governor of Virginia. Pineapples, first discovered by Europeans when Christopher Columbus landed in Guadeloupe, had been grown in glass hothouses (long vanished) in the walled garden at Dunmore, and the giant pineapple was a special homecoming of sorts.

It may well have been designed by Sir William Chambers (1723–96), the Swedish-born son of a Scottish merchant, famed for his follies at Kew Gardens as much as for Somerset House and the State Coach of 1760, a glorious royal *fa-la* on wheels. It is a joy to see the Pineapple rising in considered fashion from a Palladian garden pavilion, and a delight to discover that although its base is octagonal, the domed summer room inside is circular. Leased by the Landmark Trust from the National Trust of Scotland (the Dunmore estate was broken up in 1970), today the Pineapple is available for anyone to rent as a holiday let. It is satisfying to know that it also conforms to Vitruvius's law of commodity, firmness and (sheer) delight.

Close-up detail of the stone pineapple

Index

Picture credits

Acknowledgements

'Every judgement in science', said Jacob Bronowski, 'stands on the edge of error and is personal'. The more I've learned about architecture, the more Bronowski's claim seems true of this age-old fusion of art and science. Liz Faber of Laurence King asked me to pose the 70 questions in this book, and to attempt to answer them. Gaynor Sermon saw the book into production. Thanks to both.